WORLD ENGLISH 2

SECOND EDITION

Real People • Real Places • Real Language

Kristin L. Johannsen and Rebecca Tarver Chase, Authors

Rob Jenkins, Series Editor

 NATIONAL GEOGRAPHIC LEARNING |  CENGAGE Learning·

Australia • Brazil • Japan • Korea • Mexico • Singapore • Spain • United Kingdom • United States

World English Level 2
Real People, Real Places, Real Language
Kristin L. Johannsen and Rebecca Tarver Chase, Authors
Rob Jenkins, Series Editor

Publisher: Sherrise Roehr

Executive Editor: Sarah Kenney

Senior Development Editor: Margarita Matte

Development Editor: Brenden Layte

Assistant Editor: Alison Bruno

Editorial Assistant: Patricia Giunta

Media Researcher: Leila Hishmeh

Senior Technology Product Managers: Scott Rule, Lauren Krolick

Director of Global Marketing: Ian Martin

Senior Product Marketing Manager: Caitlin Thomas

Sr. Director, ELT & World Languages: Michael Burggren

Production Manager: Daisy Sosa

Content Project Manager: Andrea Bobotas

Senior Print Buyer: Mary Beth Hennebury

Cover Designer: Aaron Opie

Art Director: Scott Baker

Creative Director: Chris Roy

Cover Image: © Jörg Dickmann

Compositor: MPS Limited

For product information and technology assistance, contact us at
Cengage Learning Customer & Sales Support, 1-800-354-9706

For permission to use material from this text or product,
submit all requests online at **cengage.com/permissions**
Further permissions questions can be emailed to
permissionrequest@cengage.com

World English 2 ISBN: 978-1-285-84870-9
World English 2 + CD-ROM ISBN: 978-1-285-84836-5
World English 2 + Online Workbook ISBN: 978-1-305-08953-2

National Geographic Learning
20 Channel Center Street
Boston, MA 02210
USA

Cengage Learning is a leading provider of customized learning solutions with office locations around the globe, including Singapore, the United Kingdom, Australia, Mexico, Brazil, and Japan.

Cengage Learning products are represented in Canada by Nelson Education, Ltd.

Visit National Geographic Learning online at ngl.cengage.com

Visit our corporate website at www.cengage.com

Printed in the United States of America
Print Number: 08   Print Year: 2017

Thank you to the educators who provided invaluable feedback during the development of the second edition of the *World English* series:

AMERICAS

Brazil

Renata Cardoso, Universidade de Brasília, Brasília
Gladys De Sousa, Universidade Federal de Minas Gerais, Belo Horizonte
Marilena Fernandes, Associação Alumni, São Paulo
Mary Ruth Popov, Ingles Express, Ltda., Belo Horizonte
Ana Rosa, Speed, Vila Velha
Danny Sheps, English4u2, Natal
Renata Zainotte, Go Up Idiomas, Rio de Janeiro

Colombia

Eida Caicedo, Universidad de San Buenaventura Cali, Cali
Andres Felipe Echeverri Patiño, Corporación Universitaria Lasallista, Envigado
Luz Libia Rey, Centro Colombo Americano, Bogota

Dominican Republic

Aida Rosales, Instituto Cultural Dominico-Americano, Santo Domingo

Ecuador

Elizabeth Ortiz, COPEI-Copol English Institute, Guayaquil

Mexico

Ramon Aguilar, LEC Languages and Education Consulting, Hermosillo
Claudia García-Moreno Ávila, Universidad Autónoma del Estado de México, Toluca
Ana María Benton, Universidad Anahuac Mexico Norte, Huixquilucan
Martha Del Angel, Tecnológico de Monterrey, Monterrey
Sachenka García B., Universidad Kino, Hermosillo
Cinthia I. Navarrete García, Universidad Autónoma del Estado de México, Toluca
Alonso Gaxiola, Universidad Autonoma de Sinaloa, Guasave
Raquel Hernandez, Tecnológico de Monterrey, Monterrey
Beatriz Cuenca Hernández, Universidad Autónoma del Estado de México, Toluca
Luz María Lara Hernández, Universidad Autónoma del Estado de México, Toluca
Esthela Ramírez Hernández, Universidad Autónoma del Estado de México, Toluca
Ma Guadalupe Peña Huerta, Universidad Autónoma del Estado de México, Toluca
Elsa Iruegas, Prepa Tec Campus Cumbres, Monterrey
María del Carmen Turral Maya, Universidad Autónoma del Estado de México, Toluca
Lima Melani Ayala Olvera, Universidad Autónoma del Estado de México, Toluca
Suraya Ordorica Reyes, Universidad Autónoma del Estado de México, Toluca
Leonor Rosales, Tecnológico de Monterrey, Monterrey
Leticia Adelina Ruiz Guerrero, ITESO, Jesuit University, Tlaquepaque

United States

Nancy Alaks, College of DuPage, Glen Ellyn, IL
Annette Barker, College of DuPage, Aurora, IL
Joyce Gatto, College of Lake County, Grayslake, IL
Donna Glade-Tau, Harper College, Palatine, IL
Mary "Katie" Hu, Lone Star College – North Harris, Houston, TX
Christy Naghitorabi, University of South Florida, St. Petersburg, FL

ASIA

Beri Ali, Cleverlearn (American Academy), Ho Chi Minh City
Ronald Anderson, Chonnam National University, Yeosu Campus, Jeollanam
Michael Brown, Canadian Secondary Wenzhou No. 22 School, Wenzhou
Leyi Cao, Macau University of Science and Technology, Macau
Maneerat Chuaychoowong, Mae Fah Luang University, Chiang Rai
Sooah Chung, Hwarang Elementary School, Seoul
Edgar Du, Vanung University, Taoyuan County
David Fairweather, Asahikawa Daigaku, Asahikawa
Andrew Garth, Chonnam National University, Yeosu Campus, Jeollanam
Brian Gaynor, Muroran Institute of Technology, Muroran-shi
Emma Gould, Chonnam National University, Yeosu Campus, Jeollanam
David Grant, Kochi National College of Technology, Nankoku
Michael Halloran, Chonnam National University, Yeosu Campus, Jeollanam
Nina Ainun Hamdan, University Malaysia, Kuala Lumpur
Richard Hatcher, Chonnam National University, Yeosu Campus, Jeollanam
Edward Tze-Lu Ho, Chihlee Institute of Technology, New Taipei City
Soontae Hong, Yonsei University, Seoul
Chaiyathip Katsura, Mae Fah Luang University, Chiang Rai
Byoug-Kyo Lee, Yonsei University, Seoul
Han Li, Aceleader International Language Center, Beijing
Michael McGuire, Kansai Gaidai University, Osaka
Yu Jin Ng, Universiti Tenaga Nasional, Kajang, Selangor
Somaly Pan, Royal University of Phnom Penh, Phnom Penh
HyunSuk Park, Halla University, Wonju
Bunroeun Pich, Build Bright University, Phnom Penh
Renee Sawazaki, Surugadai University, Annaka-shi
Adam Schofield, Cleverlearn (American Academy), Ho Chi Minh City
Pawadee Srisang, Burapha University, Chanthaburi Campus, Ta-Mai District
Douglas Sweetlove, Kinjo Gakuin University, Nagoya
Tari Lee Sykes, National Taiwan University of Science and Technology, Taipei
Monika Szirmai, Hiroshima International University, Hiroshima
Sherry Wen, Yan Ping High School, Taipei
Chris Wilson, Okinawa University, Naha City, Okinawa
Christopher Wood, Meijo University, Nagoya
Evelyn Wu, Minghsin University of Science and Technology, Xinfeng, Hsinchu County
Aroma Xiang, Macau University of Science and Technology, Macau
Zoe Xie, Macau University of Science and Technology, Macau
Juan Xu, Macau University of Science and Technology, Macau
Florence Yap, Chang Gung University, Taoyuan
Sukanda Yatprom, Mae Fah Luang University, Chiang Rai
Echo Yu, Macau University of Science and Technology, Macau

The publisher would like to extend a special thank you to Raúl Billini, English Coordinator, Mi Colegio, Dominican Republic, for his contributions to the series.

BACKGROUND – LEARNING AND INSTRUCTION

Learning has been described as acquiring knowledge. Obtaining knowledge does not guarantee understanding, however. A math student, for example, could replicate any number of algebraic formulas, but never come to an *understanding* of how they could be used or for what purpose he or she has learned them. If understanding is defined as the ability to use knowledge, then learning could be defined differently and more accurately. The ability of the student to use knowledge instead of merely receiving information therefore becomes the goal and the standard by which learning is assessed.

This revelation has led to classrooms that are no longer teacher-centric or lecture driven. Instead, students are asked to think, ponder, and make decisions based on the information received or, even more productive, students are asked to construct learning or discover information in personal pursuits, or with help from an instructor, with partners, or in groups. The practice they get from such approaches stimulates learning with a purpose. The purpose becomes a tangible goal or objective that provides opportunities for students to transfer skills and experiences to future learning.

In the context of language development, this approach becomes essential to real learning and understanding. Learning a language is a skill that is developed only after significant practice. Students can learn the mechanics of a language but when confronted with real-world situations, they are not capable of communication. Therefore, it might be better to shift the discussion from "Language Learning" to "Communication Building." Communication should not be limited to only the productive skills. Reading and listening serve important avenues for communication as well.

FOUR PRINCIPLES TO DEVELOPING LEARNING ENVIRONMENTS

Mission: The goal or mission of a language course might adequately be stated as the pursuit of providing sufficient information and practice to allow students to communicate accurately and effectively to a reasonable extent given the level, student experiences, and time on task provided. This goal can be reflected in potential student learning outcomes identified by what students will be able to do through performance indicators.

World English provides a clear chart within the table of contents to show the expected outcomes of the course. The books are designed to capture student imagination and allow students ample opportunities to communicate. A study of the table of contents identifies the process of communication building that will go on during the course.

Context: It is important to identify what vehicle will be used to provide instruction. If students are to learn through practice, language cannot be introduced as isolated verb forms, nouns, and modifiers. It must have context. To reach the learners and to provide opportunities to communicate, the context must be interesting and relevant to learners' lives and expectations. In other words, there must be a purpose and students must have a clear understanding of what that purpose is.

World English provides a meaningful context that allows students to connect with the world. Research has demonstrated pictures and illustrations are best suited for creating interest and motivation within learners. National Geographic has a long history of providing magnificent learning environments through pictures, illustrations, true accounts, and video. The pictures, stories, and video capture the learners' imagination and "hook" them to learning in such a way that students have significant reasons to communicate promoting interaction and critical thinking. The context will also present students with a desire to know more, leading to life-long learning.

Objectives (Goals)

With the understanding that a purpose for communicating is essential, identifying precisely what the purpose is in each instance becomes crucial even before specifics of instruction have been defined. This is often called "backward design." Backward design means, in the context of classroom lesson planning, that first desired outcomes, goals, or objectives are defined and then lessons are mapped out with the end in mind, the end being what students will be able to do after sufficient instruction and practice. Having well-crafted objectives or goals provides the standard by which learners' performance can be assessed or self-assessed.

World English lessons are designed on two-page spreads so students can easily see what is expected and what the context is. The goal that directly relates to the final application activity is identified at the beginning. Students, as well as instructors, can easily evaluate their performance as they attempt the final activity. Students can also readily see what tools they will practice to prepare them for the application activity. The application activity is a task where students can demonstrate their ability to perform what the lesson goal requires. This information provides direction and purpose for the learner. Students, who know what is expected, where they are going, and how they will get there, are more apt to reach success. Each success builds confidence and additional communication skills.

Tools and Skills

Once the lesson objective has been identified and a context established, the lesson developer must choose the tools the learner will need to successfully perform the task or objective. The developer can choose among various areas in communication building including vocabulary, grammar and pronunciation. The developer must also choose skills and strategies including reading, writing, listening, and speaking. The receptive skills of reading and listening are essential components to communication. All of these tools and skills must be placed in a balanced way into a context providing practice that can be transferred to their final application or learner demonstration which ultimately becomes evidence of communication building.

World English units are divided into "lessons" that each consists of a two-page spread. Each spread focuses on different skills and strategies and is labeled by a letter (A-E). The units contain the following lesson sequence:

> A: Vocabulary
> B: Listening and Pronunciation
> C: Language Expansion
> D: Reading/Writing
> E: Video Journal

Additional grammar and vocabulary are introduced as tools throughout to provide practice for the final application activity. Each activity in a page spread has the purpose of developing adequate skills to perform the final application task.

LAST WORD

The philosophy of *World English* is to provide motivating context to connect students to the world through which they build communication skills. These skills are developed, practiced, and assessed from lesson to lesson through initially identifying the objective and giving learners the tools they need to complete a final application task. The concept of performance is highlighted over merely learning new information and performance comes from communicating about meaningful and useful context. An accumulation of small communication skills leads to true and effective communication outside of the classroom in real-world environments.

Rob Jenkins, Series Editor

	Unit Goals	Grammar	Vocabulary

UNIT 1 Food from the Earth Page 2	• Contrast general and current actions
	• Describe geography, climate, and food
	• Describe favorite dishes
	• Describe a favorite food
		Verb tense review:
		Simple present tense vs. present continuous tense
		   I **eat** rice every day.
		   She**'s cooking** fish now.
		Simple past tense (regular and irregular)
		   We **learned** how to make pizza yesterday.
			Geographical regions
			Climate
			Food staples

UNIT 2 Express Yourself Page 14	• Talk about personal experiences
	• Make small talk with new people
	• Use small talk to *break the ice*
	• Learn to overcome a language barrier
		Present perfect tense
		   He **has traveled** to many countries.
		Already, ever, never and *yet* + the present perfect tense
		   Have you **ever seen** a giraffe?
			Culture, communication, and gestures
			Small talk

UNIT 3 Cities Page 26	• Describe your city or town
	• Explain what makes a good neighborhood
	• Discuss an action plan
	• Make predictions about cities in the future
		Future with *will*
		   The city **will be** cleaner.
		Will + time clauses
		   I**'ll** check out the neighborhood **before** I rent an apartment.
			City life
			Maps

TEDTALKS   Video   Page 38   **Charlie Todd: The Shared Experience of Absurdity**

	Unit Goals	Grammar	Vocabulary

UNIT 4 The Body Page 42	• Discuss ways to stay healthy
	• Talk about lifestyles
	• Suggest helpful natural remedies
	• Explain cause and effect
		The comparatives, superlatives, and equatives
		   Henry is **healthier than** his father.
		Infinitive of purpose
		   You can drink tea with honey **to help** a sore throat.
			Human organs
			Parts of the body
			Everyday ailments

UNIT 5 Challenges Page 54	• Talk about facing challenges
	• Discuss past accomplishments
	• Use *too* and *enough* to talk about abilities
	• Describe a personal challenge
		Past continuous vs. the simple past
		   I saw him yesterday. He was riding a bike.
		Past continuous with the simple past
		   We **were eating** dinner **when you called.**
		Enough, not enough, too + adjective
		   He was **old enough** to sail alone.
			Physical and mental challenges
			Phrasal verbs

UNIT 6 Transitions Page 66	• Talk about milestones in your life
	• Talk about the best age to do something
	• Use *how* questions to get more information
	• Describe an important transition in your life
		Using the present perfect tense
		   I**'ve lived** alone for five years now.
		How + adjective or adverb
		   How tall is he?
			Stages of life
			Adjectives for age

TEDTALKS   Video   Page 78   **Hans Rosling: The Magic Washing Machine**

Listening	Speaking and Pronunciation	Reading	Writing	Video Journal
Focused listening An interview: 　Rice farming	Comparing different regions: 　discussing their climate 　and their food Linking sounds: 　final consonant followed 　by a vowel	**National Geographic:** "A Slice of History"	Responding to an e-mail	**National Geographic:** "Forbidden Fruit"
General listening Conversations: 　Small talk	Talking about what you have or haven't done Making small talk *Have* or *has* vs. contractions	**National Geographic:** "Taking Pictures of the World"	Writing opinions	**National Geographic:** "Orangutan Language"
General and focused listening A radio interview: 　Jardin Nomade in Paris	Discussing good and bad elements in a neighborhood Predicting the future of cities Emphatic stress	**TED**TALKS "How Food Shapes Our Cities"	Writing a paragraph with predictions about cities in the future	**National Geographic:** "Fes"
Focused listening Discussions: 　Different lifestyles	Talking about food and exercise that are good for you Suggesting easy remedies Linking with comparatives and superlatives	**National Geographic:** "Tiny Invaders"	Writing an excuse for a sick child	**National Geographic:** "The Human Body"
General listening An interview: 　Jenny Daltry, herpetologist	Discussing challenges Talking about abilities Words that end in *–ed*	**National Geographic:** "Arctic Dreams and Nightmares"	Writing a paragraph about a challenging experience	**National Geographic:** "Searching for the Snow Leopard"
General and focused listening A radio program: 　Healthy tips from an 　Okinawan centenarian	Talking about something you did Discussing the best age for life transitions The schwa sound /ə/ in unstressed syllables	**TED**TALKS "Living Beyond Limits"	Writing a paragraph to describe a life transition	**National Geographic:** "Nubian Wedding"

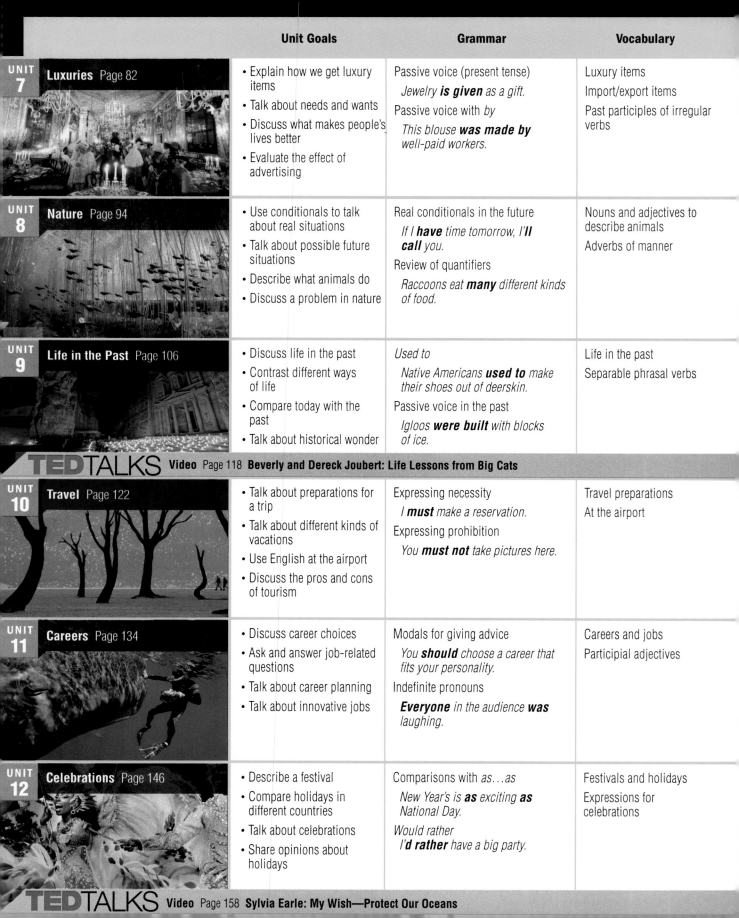

Listening	Speaking and Pronunciation	Reading	Writing	Video Journal
Focused listening Discussions: The world flower market	Discussing luxuries and necessities Talking about improving your life Sentence stress—content words vs. function words	**National Geographic:** "Perfume: The Essence of Illusion"	Writing a print ad	**National Geographic:** "Coober Pedy Opals"
General and focused listening A radio program: The bluefin tuna	Talk about issues that affect nature Role-playing to promote environmental action to make oceans sustainable Phrases in sentences	**TED**TALKS "How Poachers Became Caretakers"	Writing a paragraph to give an opinion	**National Geographic:** "Happy Elephants"
General and focused listening A lecture: The Sami people	Talking about how technology has changed our lives Discussing daily life in the past Reduction of *used to*	**National Geographic:** "Lord of the Mongols"	Writing a paragraph on one of the New 7 Wonders of the World	**National Geographic:** "Searching for Genghis Khan"
General and focused listening Conversations: Vacations	Planning a dream vacation Making your way through the airport Reduction of *have to, has to, got to*	**National Geographic:** "Tourists or Trees?"	Writing a paragraph about how tourists can help a place they visit	**National Geographic:** "Adventure Capital of the World"
General and focused listening An interview: A restaurant owner in Thailand	Discussing career choices Intonation in questions	**TED**TALKS "Making Filthy Water Drinkable"	Writing a letter giving advice	**National Geographic:** "Trinidad Bird Man"
General and focused listening Discussions: Local celebrations or holidays	Comparing different international celebrations Talking about personal celebrations Question intonation with lists	**National Geographic:** "Starting a New Tradition"	Writing a substantiated opinion	**National Geographic:** "Young Riders of Mongolia"

Heirloom carrots sold in a farmer's market

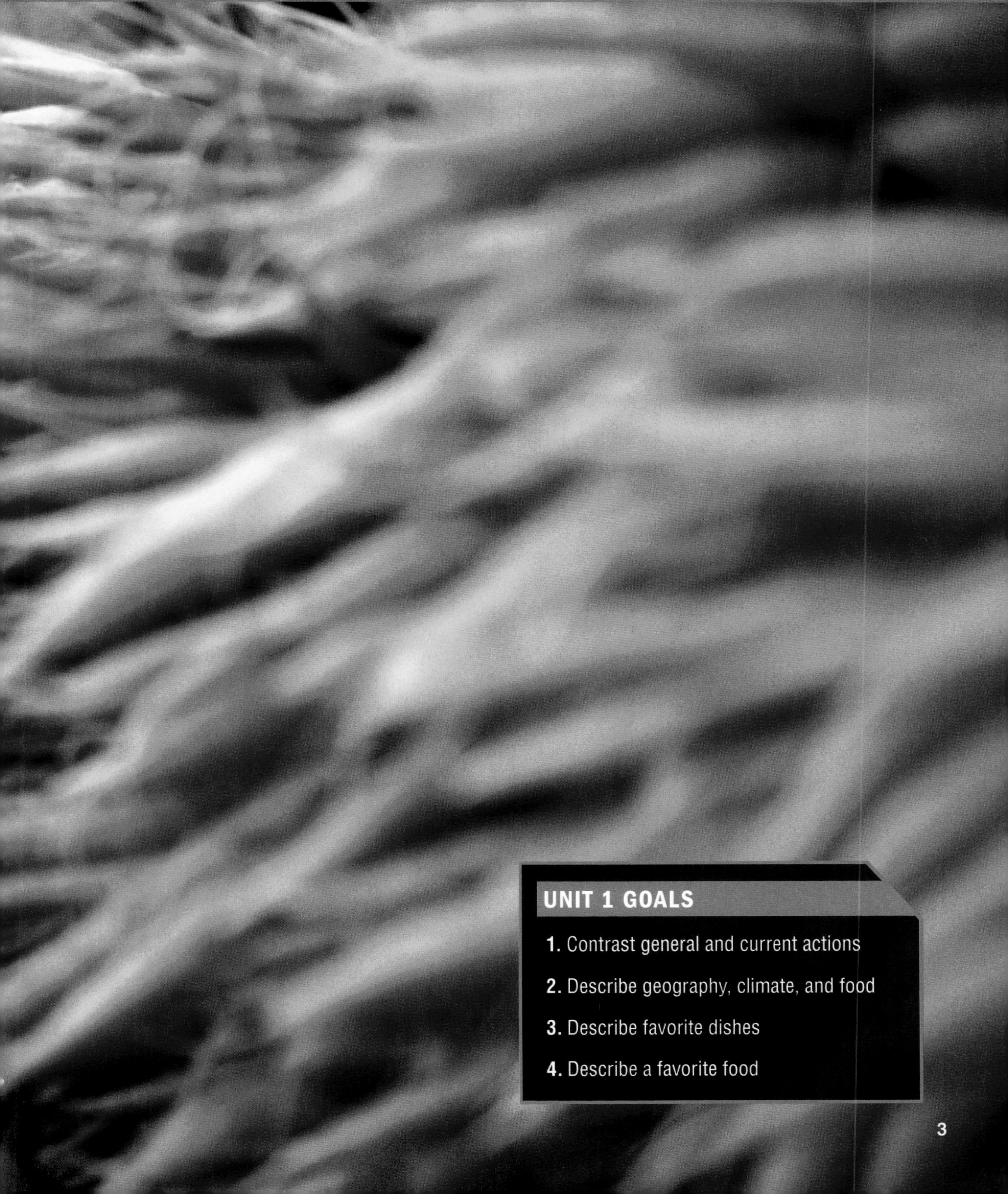

UNIT 1 GOALS

1. Contrast general and current actions

2. Describe geography, climate, and food

3. Describe favorite dishes

4. Describe a favorite food

▲ Armenian church on Akdamar island, Turkey

Vocabulary

A Read part of a travel blog.

This is my first visit to Turkey. It's a wonderful place! The people are friendly and the meals are delicious. Farmers here grow many different crops, including many kinds of fruit. They also grow a lot of wheat, and the bread in Turkey is really good. Of course, the geography and climate in different parts of Turkey affect the kind of food farmers can produce in each region. In Central Anatolia, the land is almost flat, and the weather is usually warm and dry. It's a good place to grow crops and to raise animals such as cattle and sheep. High up in the mountains of eastern Turkey, farmers also keep animals since they can't grow crops. Today I'm visiting the coast of the Mediterranean Sea in southern Turkey. The weather here is hot and humid, but the fish and seafood are excellent!

B Write the words in blue next to the correct meaning.

1. _____ people who produce food

2. _____ an area of a country or of the world

3. _____ plants grown for food

4. _____ very high parts of the land

5. _____ describes air with a lot of water in it

6. _____ land near the ocean

7. _____ describes land without mountains

8. _____ features of a place, such as rivers

9. _____ breakfast, lunch, and dinner

10. _____ normal weather in a certain place

Grammar: Simple present vs. present continuous tense

Simple present tense		Present continuous tense	
I **eat** rice She **cooks** fish They **bake** bread We **have** fruit for breakfast	every day.	I'm **eating** rice She's **cooking** fish They**'re baking** bread We**'re having** mangos for breakfast	now.
*Use the simple present tense to talk about habits and things that are generally true. *Use the present continuous tense to talk about actions and events that are happening now.			

A Complete each sentence with the simple present or present continuous form of the verb in parentheses.

1. My mother and I _____ a meal together every afternoon. (cook)

2. In Mexico, most people _____ a big meal in the afternoon. (eat)

3. Right now, my mother and I _____ a dish called *enchiladas*. (make)

4. I really like enchiladas. Sometimes I _____ them for breakfast! (have)

5. Now my mother _____ the whole family to come to the table. (tell)

6. We _____ at least one meal together every day. (enjoy)

B Take turns with a partner doing the following.

1. Tell your partner what you usually eat for breakfast and lunch. (Use the simple present tense.)

2. Tell your partner three things people you know are doing right now. (Use the present continuous tense.)

▲ Enchiladas with rice

Conversation

A 🔊 2 Close your book and listen to the conversation. What do Julie's cousins usually eat?

Tom: What are you doing?

Julie: I'm looking at pictures from my vacation.

Tom: Oh, can I see? Where did you go?

Julie: I visited my cousins in the south. It's very flat there—no mountains or hills, and it's pretty dry for most of the year.

Tom: What about food? What do your cousins usually eat?

Julie: Meals are very simple there. It's basically meat and potatoes and a lot of vegetables. But they grow wheat everywhere, so pasta is becoming popular.

Tom: That sounds good.

Julie: Yes, I really like the food there.

B Practice the conversation with a partner. Switch roles and practice it again.

C How is the geography and food in your part of the world similar to or different from the place Julie describes? Work in small groups and share your answers to the question.

> I usually wear glasses, but today I'm wearing contact lenses.

D **GOAL CHECK** ✔ **Contrast general and current actions**

Complete this sentence three times. Two of the sentences should be true, but one should be untrue: *I usually _____ , but today I'm _____ .*

Read your sentences to your partner in any order. Your partner will guess which sentence is false.

> And I usually carry my phone to class, but today I'm letting my sister use my phone.

▲ People working in a rice paddy.

Word Focus

Farmers **raise crops** or **grow crops.**

Engage!

Do you think farmers and scientists need to find ways to increase food production? Why?

Listening

A 🔁 Look at the picture. Discuss these questions with a partner.

1. What are important foods that everyone in your country eats?
2. Where in the world do farmers grow rice?
3. Why do they grow it there?

B 🔊 3 Listen to the interview. Circle the correct letter.

1. Who is the interviewer talking to?

   a. a restaurant owner   **b.** a rice farmer   **c.** a news reporter

2. What is happening in the rice paddy today? People are . . .

   a. planting rice plants.   **b.** planting seeds.   **c.** letting water into the paddy.

3. What kind of climate does rice need?

   a. hot and dry   **b.** warm and wet   **c.** cool and humid

C 🔊 3 Listen again and answer the questions.

1. Why doesn't the rice farmer plant seeds like other farmers?

   _____

2. How is the rainfall this year? _____

3. What happens to the water in the rice paddy after the rice plants grow?

   _____

4. What happens to the rice plants after they're dry? _____

Communication

A 🔁 Talk with a partner about two different regions in your country. Describe the land, the climate, and the food.

	Region #1	Region #2
land		
climate		
staple foods		

B 🔗 Get together with another pair of students. Describe your two regions and have the other students guess the names of the regions.

A Welsh fisherman rakes the sand to harvest small shellfish.

Pronunciation: Linking words together

When a word ends in a consonant sound, and the next word starts with a vowel sound, the words are linked together.

We cut the rice plants and clean them.   **We grow a lot of rice.**

A 🔊 4 Listen to the sentences. Notice the pronunciation of the linked words. Listen again and repeat the sentences.

1. I usually like a tomato with breakfast.
2. Staple foods are the most important foods.
3. We're eating dinner now.
4. Paul and I don't like fish very much.
5. Farmers work on weekends and holidays.
6. Rain falls in all regions of the world.

B 🔄 Underline the sounds that link together. Then read the sentences to a partner.

1. Hal enjoys pizza.
2. Wheat bread is very popular.
3. Corn grows well in Mexico.
4. A ham and cheese sandwich is my favorite lunch.
5. My friend is eating sushi.
6. Dry grasslands are good places to raise animals.

C 🔄 **GOAL CHECK** ✓ **Describe geography, climate, and food**

Tell a partner about your ideal place. It can be a real or imagined place. Describe the geography and climate there as well as the food people usually eat.

Language Expansion: Staple food crops

A What do you know about staple food crops? Circle **T** for *true* or **F** for *false*.

1.	Potatoes are originally from South America.	**T**	**F**
2.	India is one of the world's largest producers of wheat.	**T**	**F**
3.	Lentils are a kind of legume.	**T**	**F**
4.	Soy sauce is made from soybeans.	**T**	**F**
5.	Yucca grows in (under) the ground.	**T**	**F**
6.	China is the world's largest consumer of rice.	**T**	**F**

B 🗣 Discuss the questions with a partner.

1. In what parts of the world do people eat these staple foods?
2. What other staple foods do you know about?
3. What staple foods do you usually eat?

> **People eat a lot of soybeans in Asian countries.**

> **Right, or they eat foods made from soybeans, like *tofu* and *miso*.**

Word Focus

With the simple past, we often use:

yesterday/the day before **yesterday**

days/weeks/years/months **ago**

last week/month/year

Engage!

Write sentences about your own life in a notebook. Use the simple past and words from the grammar chart, for example: *I **ate** sushi at a party last month, and I liked it!*

Grammar: Simple past tense

Simple past tense	
We **learned** how to make pizza Too much rain **fell** I **ate** sushi for the first time	yesterday. last November. in 2006.
*Some verbs are regular in the simple past tense. They have an *-ed* ending.	*Some verbs are irregular in the simple past tense. They have many different forms.
learn – learned want – wanted arrive – arrived need – needed play – played help – helped ask – asked show – showed travel – traveled	see – saw take – took eat – ate fall – fell drink – drank try – tried go – went meet – met send – sent be – was/were give – gave

A Complete the conversation. Use the simple past tense of the verbs in parentheses.

Mary: Tell me about yourself, Pedro.

Pedro: Well, I love to travel. Last year I _____ (travel) to Greece.

Mary: Wow! You _____ (go) to Greece?

Pedro: Yes, and I _____ (meet) my friend Vasilys and his family there.

They _____ (show) me around Athens and _____ (introduce) me to many new foods.

Mary: That sounds like fun.

Pedro: It was. I _____ (eat) seafood and lamb, and I _____ (try) a dish made from rice and grape leaves. It _____ (be) delicious!

B Complete these sentences about the past. Use your own information.

1. Yesterday, I ate _____.

2. Last week, I went _____.

3. On the first day of this class, I learned _____.

4. Last month, _____.

5. In 2012, _____.

6. Ten years ago, _____.

Real Language

When we say something is *made from* other things, we're talking about its ingredients.

Conversation

A 🔊 **5** Close your book and listen to the conversation. What is Albert eating? What is it made from?

Albert: You should try this! My aunt made it.

Mary: Mmmm . . . Delicious! What is it?

Albert: It's called *couscous*. It's made from wheat.

Mary: And what's this on top of the couscous?

Albert: Mostly vegetables and some kind of sauce.

Mary: How did your aunt learn to cook it?

Albert: Her great-uncle married a woman from North Africa. That's where couscous is from. They always ate it on special occasions.

Mary: What an interesting family history!

Albert: Yeah, and a great family recipe.

▲ North African couscous

B 🔁 Practice the conversation. Switch roles and practice it again. Tell your partner about some foods you like that come from other parts of the world.

C 🔁 **GOAL CHECK** ✔ Describe favorite dishes

Look at the staple foods on page 8. Tell your partner about dishes you like to eat that are made with these staple foods. When was the last time you ate each dish?

> I really like Indian *biryani*. It's a rice dish with vegetables and spices. I ate it last month at a restaurant.

Reading

A Read the title and the first sentence of each paragraph. How is the reading organized?

    a. by importance, from least important to most important

    b. over time, from earliest to latest

    c. comparison and contrast, showing similarities and differences

B Read the whole article and complete each sentence.

    1. People thousands of years ago made flat bread on hot _____.

    2. _____ people ate tomatoes before European people.

    3. Cooks in _____ put tomatoes on flat bread.

    4. _____ brought pizza to the United States.

    5. People eat lamb and tofu on pizza in _____.

C Make a list of popular foods that came from other countries. Where did these foods come from? Tell a partner.

> **People here eat a lot of curry. I think it came from India.**

> **Right. There's an Indian restaurant downtown. They have wonderful curry.**

Communication

A Work in a small group. Invent a new kind of pizza for Lombardi's restaurant. You should all agree on the toppings, the sauce, and the type of crust.

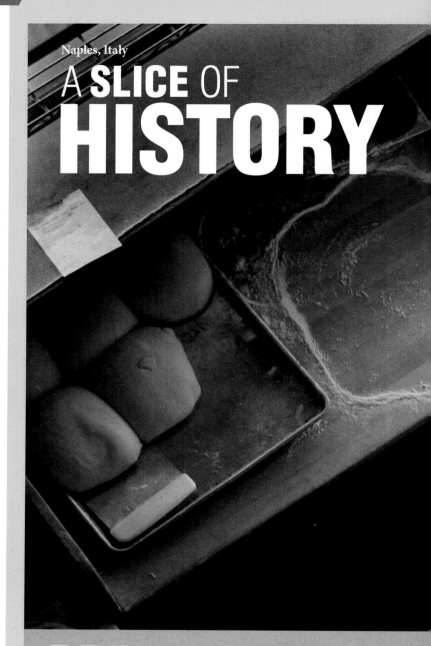

Naples, Italy

A SLICE OF HISTORY

What do you like on your pizza? Cheese? Tomatoes? Sausage? People may disagree on their favorite ingredients, but many people agree that pizza is a favorite food. Where and when did people start making pizza? To find out, we have to travel back in time.

Thousands of years ago, people used ancient types of wheat and other grains to make flat bread on the hot rocks of their **campfires.** At some point in time, early cooks started putting other kinds of food on the bread—using the bread as a plate. It was the world's first pizza **crust!**

Over time, pizza began to look more like the food we know today. When European explorers arrived in the Americas, they saw Native American people eating tomatoes. When they brought tomatoes back to Europe, however, people there wouldn't eat them. They thought eating tomatoes could make them ill.

Slowly, however, Europeans discovered that tomatoes were delicious and safe to eat. Cooks in Naples, an Italian city, began putting tomatoes on their flat bread. The world's first true pizza shop opened in Naples in 1830. People there ate pizza for lunch and dinner. They even ate it for breakfast!

In the late 1800s, many Italians moved to the United States. They brought pizza with them. The first American pizzeria, or pizza restaurant, was Lombardi's in New York City. It opened its doors in 1905. Now pizza is one of the three most popular foods in the USA, but Americans are not the only pizza lovers.

People now eat around five billion pizzas a year, and everyone has their favorite kind. Brazilians love green peas on their pizza. Russians like fish and onions. People in India use lamb and tofu. The Japanese think seafood on pizza is good. Some pizzas truly sound **strange,** yet all of them share two things. Each begins with bread. And each is a **slice** of history.

Food vendor at the Damnoen Saduak Floating Market in Thailand.

Writing

A Read the email and write a response. Be sure to answer all the questions.

From: Ronald Ferguson

To: _____

Subject: Help! My students have some questions for you.

Hi there,

How is everything there? I hope you're doing well, and I hope you can answer some questions from my students. Our class will visit your country next month, and the students are asking me about the food. Here are some of their questions:

What do people usually eat for breakfast there?
Do you have pizza and hamburger restaurants?
What are some traditional dishes we can try?

Is there a staple food that people eat every day?
What are some good things to eat for lunch and dinner?

Thank you very much! I look forward to our visit next month. Maybe you can join us for a good meal.

Your friend,
Ronald

Communication

A Share your e-mail with a partner. Did your partner answer all of Ronald Ferguson's questions? Did you and your partner answer any of the questions differently?

B **GOAL CHECK** ✔ **Describe a favorite food**

Discuss the questions with a partner.

1. What foods from your country are now popular in other places?

2. Why do you think people like these foods?

a floating market

Before You Watch

A 🔄 Discuss the following questions with a partner. Use the adjectives in the box.

1. What are some foods that have a very strong smell?

2. After you prepare food with a strong smell in your home, how can you get rid of the odor?

> smelly   delicious
> fragrant   disgusting

While You Watch

A ▶ Watch the video *Forbidden Fruit*. Match the people to the actions.

1. Hotel staff _____

2. Hotel guests _____

3. Hotel cleaning staff _____

a. try to bring durian fruit into hotel rooms.

b. use a special machine in smelly hotel rooms.

c. watch for people bringing in durian fruit.

B ▶ Watch the video again and write the correct answer.

1. How old are durian trees when they begin to produce fruit? _____

2. How many American dollars can one durian fruit cost? _____

3. Where do hotel owners want people to eat durian fruit? _____

After You Watch / Communication

A 🔄 Write a guide for tourists visiting your country. Describe three foods that are popular in your culture, but that people from other cultures might find disgusting or intolerable. Give reasons why tourists should try those foods.

▲ Durian fruit

B 🔗 You are a group of hotel owners in Malaysian Borneo. Brainstorm a list of ways to prevent people from bringing durian fruit into their hotel rooms.

Crane workers on a construction site

Look at the photo, answer the questions:

1 What are the people probably talking about?

2 Who do you talk with every day?

UNIT 2 GOALS

1. Talk about personal experiences

2. Make small talk with new people

3. Use small talk to *break the ice*

4. Learn to overcome a language barrier

▲ A photographer talks with a Nepalese woman.

Vocabulary

A Read the article.

Every culture around the world has different customs and ways of communicating. When you learn a language, you learn more than words. You also learn a lot of rules. You learn what kind of greetings to use in different situations. For example, in English, we use formal and informal greetings. In China, a traditional greeting is "Have you eaten today?" In addition, there are rules for making small talk when you meet a person. Once you have learned the rules of a language, you can communicate more easily and avoid misunderstandings.

People in different cultures also have different ways of using their bodies to communicate. We use our heads and our hands to make gestures, for example. But there's one kind of communication that's the same everywhere. A smile can always connect people.

B Write the words in blue next to the correct meaning.

1. _____ instructions for what is allowed

2. _____ happy facial expression

3. _____ movements used to communicate

4. _____ to join together

5. _____ behaviors special to a country or people

6. _____ problems caused when one is not understood

7. _____ usual ways of doing things

8. _____ informal talk about everyday topics

9. _____ describes customs from long ago

10. _____ language used when we meet someone

Grammar: Present perfect tense

Present perfect tense
Subject + **has/have** + **(not)** + **past participle** He **has traveled** to many countries. He **has not been** in Korea before.
We use the present perfect tense: *to talk about something that started in the past and continues now. *to talk about something that happened several times in the past. *to talk about something in the past that is connected with the present.

A Complete the sentences. Use the present perfect form of the verb in parentheses.

1. I _____ (meet) many Canadians, but I _____ (not, be) to Canada.

2. Jason doesn't want to watch a movie tonight. He _____ (watch) movies every night for the past week.

3. Sam _____ (travel) to Argentina four times. He loves it there!

4. My husband and I _____ (be) married for six years.

5. It's my friend's birthday, but I _____ (not, buy) her a present yet!

6. I think Lee will do well on the test. He _____ (study) a lot for it.

B Complete the questions. Ask a partner to answer them. Write some questions of your own in your notebook.

Have you ever . . .

1. eaten _____ food?

2. seen a movie from _____ (country)?

3. gone to _____ ?

4. played _____ ?

5. talked to _____ ?

> **Have you ever eaten Indian food?**
>
> **No, never.**
>
> **Yes, once/many times. It's really good!**

Real Language

We use *Guess what?* in informal conversations to say that we have interesting news.

Conversation

A 🔊 **6** Close your book and listen to the conversation. Why is the woman worried?

Annie: Guess what? I'm going to spend a month in Mexico City.

Rick: That's great! What are you going to do there?

Annie: I'm going to work in my company's office there. I'm a little worried, though. I've never been to Mexico before.

Rick: But you've met lots of people from Mexico, and you've taken Spanish lessons.

Annie: That's true. And I guess I've learned something about Mexican customs.

Rick: It sounds to me like you're ready to go.

B Practice the conversation with a partner. Switch roles and practice it again. Tell your partner how you might feel about going to another country.

C **GOAL CHECK** ✓ **Talk about personal experiences**

Which of these things have you done or not done? Use the present perfect to tell a partner about your experiences.

talk to someone from another culture   speak a foreign language

communicate with gestures   make small talk with a stranger

▲ Palace of Bellas Artes, Mexico City

Listening

A 🔊 **7** These people are meeting for the first time. Listen to their conversations. Where are the people?

Conversation 1 The speakers are in _____ .
   a. a hospital   **b.** a school   **c.** an airport

Conversation 2 These people are in _____ .
   a. a restaurant   **b.** an apartment   **c.** an office building

B 🔊 **7** Listen again. What do the people make small talk about?

Conversation 1 They make small talk about _____ .
   a. classes   **b.** weather   **c.** clothes

Conversation 2 They make small talk about _____ .
   a. sports   **b.** TV shows   **c.** the neighborhood

C 🔄 Work with a partner. What will they talk about next? Think of two more ideas for each conversation.

Pronunciation: *Have* or *has* vs. contractions

In statements with the present perfect tense, ***have*** and ***has*** are sometimes pronounced completely, but in informal speaking, contractions may be used.

> *Remember that *has* is pronounced with a /z/ sound.
>
> She **has** already watched that movie, so she doesn't want to see it again.
>
> *Remember to link words together when the word after a contraction begins with a vowel sound.
>
> **I've always** liked that restaurant. They serve delicious food there.

A 🔊 **8** Listen and repeat.

Have	Contraction	*Has*	Contraction
I have	I've	she has	she's
you have	you've	he has	he's
we have	we've	it has	it's
they have	they've		

B 🔊 **9** Listen and circle the sentences you hear.

1. **a.** I have never gone skiing.   **b.** I've never gone skiing.
2. **a.** He has been to Colombia three times.   **b.** He's been to Colombia three times.
3. **a.** Linda has taken a scuba diving class.   **b.** Linda's taken a scuba diving class.
4. **a.** They have already eaten breakfast.   **b.** They've already eaten breakfast.
5. **a.** We have had three tests this week.   **b.** We've had three tests this week.
6. **a.** Michael has found a new job.   **b.** Michael's found a new job.

Communication

A Read the information.

English-speakers often make small talk when they meet someone new. They have a conversation to get to know the other person. In general, small talk should make people feel more comfortable—not less comfortable—so the topics should not be very personal. For example, "Which department do you work in?" is a good question at work, but "How much money do you make?" is too personal.

B Circle the topics that are good for small talk when you meet someone for the first time. Then add two more ideas. Compare your ideas.

school   money   family   work   sports   religion _____ _____

C Read the situations. Circle the best question for each situation. Then practice conversations with a partner.

Situation 1 At work, Min-Hee talks to Judy. It's Judy's first day at her job.
   a. How old are you?   **b.** Are you new in this city?

Situation 2 Andrei is from Russia. He talks to Eduardo at the International Students' Club. It's Eduardo's first meeting.
   a. Where are you from?   **b.** Do you practice a religion?

Situation 3 Mark lives in apartment 104. He meets Lisa, his new neighbor.
   a. Which apartment do you live in?   **b.** Are you married?

D Which are good questions to ask when you meet someone new? Circle the letters.

a. Which classes are you taking now?

b. Who is your teacher?

c. What was your score on the placement test?

d. Have you studied at this school before?

e. When did you start working here?

f. How much did you pay for that car?

g. Have you lived here for a long time?

h. How much money do you earn here?

E | **GOAL CHECK** ✓ **Make small talk with new people**

Pretend you are meeting your classroom partner for the first time (on the first day of class, waiting for the bus, or in another situation). Talk for two minutes.

Language Expansion: Starting a conversation

A Read the questions in the box. Think of different ways to answer them.

Starting a conversation

How do you like this weather? Are you enjoying this class?

Did you hear about _____? (something in the news, for example)

How long have you been waiting? (for the elevator, the bus, the meeting to begin, etc.)

B Choose one of the situations. Try to make small talk for as long as you can. Then change partners and practice again with another situation.

| waiting in line in the office cafeteria | walking in the park |
| at a welcome party for new students | at the airport |

Grammar: *Already, ever, never,* and *yet*

Already, ever, never, and *yet* + the present perfect		
already	Use *already* in questions and affirmative statements to emphasize that something has happened in the past.	**Has** Roberta **already left**? We **have already studied** this.
(not) yet	Use *yet/not yet* in questions or negative statements for emphasis.	**Have** you **done** the dishes **yet**? Melanie **hasn't eaten** lunch **yet**.
(not) ever *never*	Use *ever/never (not ever)* in questions or negative statements to talk about something that has or has not happened at any time before now.	**Have** you **ever** seen a giraffe? We **have never** played tennis in the rain. We **haven't ever** gone to Canada.

A Read the page from Marcy's journal. What has she already done? What has she not done yet? Complete the sentences.

1. She has already _____.

2. She has already _____.

3. She has not _____ yet.

4. _____.

Things I Want to Do in My Life

take a cooking class (✓)

visit my cousins in Colombia

learn to speak Spanish (✓)

play Australian rugby

B Read the conversation between Marcy and a classmate. Fill in each blank with one word.

John: Have you ever traveled to another country?

Marcy: No, I have _____ left this country, but I want to go to Colombia someday. Some of my cousins live there.

John: I see. Have _____ already met your Colombian cousins?

Marcy: Yes, I have _____ them. They came here last year.

John: That's nice. Are there any other countries you want to visit?

Marcy: I want to visit Australia someday. _____ you ever been there?

John: No, I haven't _____ been there. Why do you want to go?

Marcy: Well, I learned the rules for Australian rugby last year, but I _____ not played the game yet. Maybe I can play it in Australia!

C Have a conversation with your partner about things you have and haven't yet done in your life. Use small talk to break the ice first.

▲ Cathedral in Bolivar Square in Bogota, Colombia

Conversation

A 🔊 10 Close your book and listen to the conversation. What do the speakers decide to do about the homework?

Tom: Excuse me. Are you in my history class?

Rita: Yes! I saw you in class yesterday. I'm Rita.

Tom: Hi, Rita. I'm Tom. Is this your first class with Mr. Olsen?

Rita: Yes, it is, but I've heard good things about him. What about you?

Tom: I've taken his classes before, and they've always been good.

Rita: That's nice. Have you already done the homework for tomorrow?

Tom: No, not yet. What about you?

Rita: Not yet. Maybe we can call each other to talk about it.

Tom: That's a great idea! I'll give you my number.

B Practice the conversation. Then practice the conversation with subjects you are studying and teachers from your school.

C **GOAL CHECK** ✔ **Use small talk to *break the ice***

Move around the class. Walk up to five classmates and ask *icebreaker* questions.

Have you ever taken a class with Ms. Lee before?

Yes, I took an art class with her.

Reading

A 🔁 Discuss these questions with a partner.

1. Have you ever taken a picture of people you didn't know? How did you do it?

2. What kinds of photographs do you like? What makes those photographs good?

B Circle **T** for *true* or **F** for *false*. Then correct the false sentences.

1. Griffiths has never traveled to England.   **T**   **F**

2. Griffiths has never traveled to Antarctica.   **T**   **F**

3. Petra is a very old city in Jordan.   **T**   **F**

4. Griffiths can only connect with English-speakers.   **T**   **F**

5. Most people do not want Griffiths to take their picture.   **T**   **F**

6. Volunteering is one way to begin a photography career.   **T**   **F**

Communication

A 🔁 Which actions can help people from different cultures to communicate? Which actions are not helpful for communication? Talk with a partner.

smile at people you don't know	pretend to understand everything
use gestures to communicate	ask people about words in their language
say nothing if you don't know the right word	other _____

Word Focus

landscapes = broad view of the land

overwhelmed = very emotional

rewarding = a valuable experience

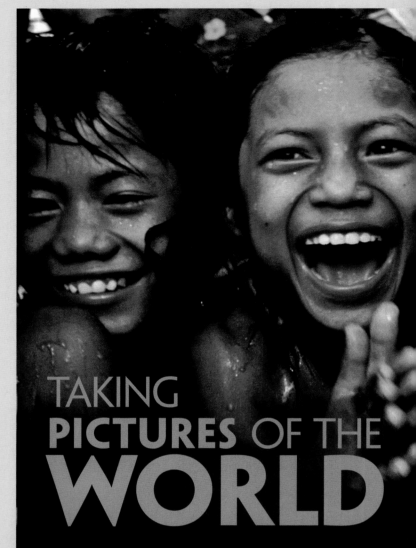

TAKING PICTURES OF THE WORLD

Meet Annie Griffiths, a National Geographic photographer. Griffiths has worked for National Geographic since 1978, and has taken pictures on almost every continent in the world. In fact, Antarctica is the only continent Griffiths hasn't seen yet.

Griffiths' photographs are well known for their beauty and high quality. They also reflect very different cultures and regions of the world. Griffiths has photographed the ancient city of Petra, Jordan, as well as the green **landscapes** of the Lake District in England. Her pictures have also appeared in a book about natural places in North America.

Everywhere that Griffiths goes, she takes pictures of people. Griffiths has found ways to connect with people of all ages and nationalities even when she does not speak their language. "The greatest privilege of my job is being allowed into people's lives," she has said. "The camera is like a passport, and I am often **overwhelmed** by how quickly people welcome me."

Portrait by Annie Griffiths

Knowing how to *break the ice* has helped to make Griffiths a successful photographer, but experts say that anyone can learn to connect with new people. When people speak the same language, greetings and small talk can make strangers feel more comfortable with each other. When people don't speak the same language, a smile is very helpful.

Griffiths has some advice if you are thinking about a career in photography. You can volunteer to take pictures for someone who can't afford to hire a professional photographer, for example. Griffiths also recommends studying and learning from good photos taken by professional photographers.

Remember, the next time you look at a beautiful photograph, you might be looking at the work of Annie Griffiths. And the next time you meet a new person, don't be afraid to break the ice. The connection you make could be very **rewarding.**

▲ Ancient acacia trees near the red sand dunes of the Namib Desert

Writing

A Complete the sentences with your own ideas.

1. Annie Griffiths' work is interesting because _____.

2. Griffiths takes good "people pictures" because _____.

3. For me, traveling is _____ because _____.

4. For me, connecting with new people is _____ because _____.

5. The next time I need to "break the ice," I will _____.

B Use your ideas from exercise **A** to complete the paragraph in your notebook.

Today I read about a National Geographic photographer. Her name is Annie Griffiths, and _____

_____

_____

Communication

Do smile at people.

Don't expect them to know your language.

A 👥 Talk to your classmates about some places you have traveled. How did you communicate with the people in those places? Then make a list of *Do's* and *Don'ts* for communicating with people who speak a different language.

B 🗣 **GOAL CHECK** ✔ **Learn to overcome a language barrier**

In what professions do people need to overcome language barriers quickly in order to do their jobs? Talk with your partner about different ways they can do this.

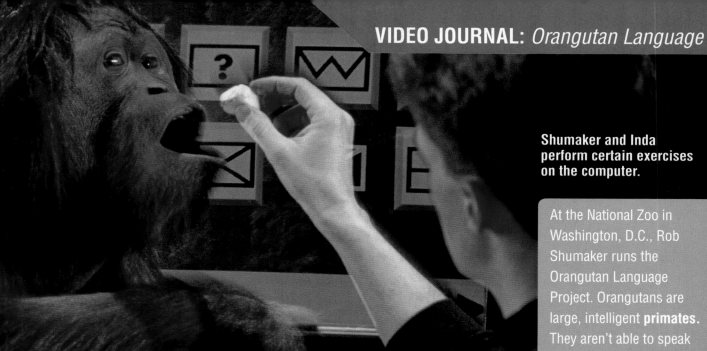

Shumaker and Inda perform certain exercises on the computer.

At the National Zoo in Washington, D.C., Rob Shumaker runs the Orangutan Language Project. Orangutans are large, intelligent **primates.** They aren't able to speak like humans, but they can learn to connect **symbols** to real objects. Shumaker believes the language program is mentally **stimulating** for the orangutans. The program is **voluntary,** so the animals can choose to participate or not. It's part of a zoo **exhibit** which educates people about the problems orangutans face in the wild.

Before You Watch

A Read about the video and look up the meanings of the words in bold.

While You Watch

A ▶ Watch the video and circle the correct answers.

1. In Malay, the word *orangutan* means "person of the (jungle | forest)."
2. The orangutans in the video are Inda and (Miki | Azie).
3. The orangutans work with symbols on (a computer | paper).
4. The orangutans are (brother and sister | mother and son).
5. Wild orangutans could become extinct in (10 to 12 | 8 to 10) years.

B ▶ Watch the video again and answer the questions in your notebook.

1. Where do orangutans come from?
2. What choices does the zoo give the orangutans?
3. How old is Inda, the female orangutan?
4. What do zoo officials hope exhibits like Think Tank will do?

After You Watch / Communication

A Brainstorm several ways that animals communicate. Do you think animal communication is very different from human communication?

B You have the opportunity to create a new way to write English. Think of ten English words that are difficult to spell. Make a word list with a better way to write the words. Share your word list with the class. (Can your classmates guess all the words?)

Cities

Japanese-inspired 'Shibuya' style
crossing at Oxford Circus in London

UNIT 3 GOALS

1. Describe your city or town

2. Explain what makes a good neighborhood

3. Discuss an action plan

4. Make predictions about cities in the future

▲ Shibuya Crossing outside Shibuya Station in Tokyo, Japan

Vocabulary

A Read the opinions. Which one do you agree with?

Opinion 1

"Urban life is great! There is good public transportation, like trains and buses. And we also have highways where cars can go fast. People can find good jobs. And after work, there is great nightlife in restaurants and dance clubs. Cities get bigger every year because they are the best places to live."

Opinion 2

"City life is terrible! Cities are so crowded, with too many people in a small area, and the population grows every year. There is too much traffic, because people want to drive everywhere. It's always noisy. A lot of people want to live in a rural area, but there aren't many jobs. It's better to live in a suburb and commute to a job by car."

B Write the words in blue next to the correct meaning.

1. _____ in the city
2. _____ roads where cars go fast
3. _____ travel to your job
4. _____ trains, buses, and subways
5. _____ number of people
6. _____ things to do in the evening
7. _____ cars moving on a street
8. _____ too full
9. _____ too loud
10. _____ in the country

Grammar: Future with *will*

A 🔁 What do you think? Circle **Y** for *yes* or **N** for *no*. Compare your answers with a partner's answers.

In the year 2030 . . .

1. My city will be bigger than it is now.   **Y**   **N**
2. People will drive cars in the city.   **Y**   **N**
3. Houses will be smaller than they are now.   **Y**   **N**
4. Cities will have many parks and green spaces.   **Y**   **N**

Word Focus

traffic jam = so many cars in the street that they can't move

population growth = more people living in a place

Will		
Statement	The city **will be** cleaner.	Use *will* to make predictions about things you are sure about in the future and to ask questions about the future. In speaking, use contractions with *will*: *I'll, you'll, he'll, she'll, we'll, they'll.*
Negative	People **won't drive** cars.	
Yes/No questions	**Will** houses **be** smaller?	
Wh- questions	Where **will** people **live**?	

B Complete the sentences and questions with a word from the box.

when   he   not
will   be

1. Silvio will _____ in New York next April for an interesting event.

2. Will _____ enjoy New York in April? It can be cold at that time.

3. The weather will _____ be a problem.

4. _____ he participate in The JFK Runway Run?

5. That's a great event. _____ will the race begin?

C 🔁 Ask a partner three questions about city life in the future. Use *will*.

Conversation

A 🔊 11 Close your book and listen to the conversation. Where did Mimi live when she was a child?

Mark: So, where are you from, Mimi?
Mimi: I live in New York now, but I grew up in Seoul.
Mark: Really? I've never been to Seoul. What's it like?
Mimi: Well, some people think it's too crowded, but it has great restaurants.
Mark: I've heard that it's very polluted.
Mimi: That's true, but it's changing now. In the future, it will be much cleaner.

> How will people commute in the future?

> I think they'll have personal airplanes!

B 🔁 Practice the conversation with a partner. Switch roles and practice it again.

C Check (✓) the things that are true about your city. Add some ideas of your own.

Bad things about your city		Good things about your city	
It's _____.		It has great _____.	
☐ noisy	☐ boring	☐ restaurants	☐ beaches
☐ dangerous	☐ crowded	☐ parks	☐ museums
☐ expensive	☐ polluted	☐ neighborhoods	☐ nightlife
_____	_____	_____	_____

D 🔁 **GOAL CHECK** ✔ **Describe your city or town**

With a partner, have a new conversation about your city. Then make new conversations about two other cities you know.

▲ Bongeunsa Temple in Seoul, South Korea

▲ The Jardin Nomade
in Paris

Listening

A 🔄 Discuss these questions with a partner.

1. How often do you go to a park?

2. What do you do there?

3. What do you think about the parks in your city or town?

B 🔊 12 Listen to a radio program about a park in Paris called the Jardin Nomade. Circle the correct letter.

1. The Jardin Nomade is in _____ area.

   a. a rural   **b.** an urban   **c.** a suburban

2. The Jardin Nomade is amazing because it's so _____.

   a. big   **b.** small   **c.** old

3. In the Jardin Nomade, people _____.

   a. grow food   **b.** go swimming   **c.** enjoy art

C 🔊 12 Listen again. Answer each question in your notebook.

1. What year did the park start? _____

2. How many gardens do people have in the park? _____

3. What do the neighbors eat there every month? _____

4. How many people come to the monthly dinners? _____

5. How many parks like this are there in Paris now? _____

Pronunciation: Emphatic stress

A 🔊 13 Listen and repeat the exchanges. Notice how the underlined words sound stronger.

1. **A:** Is your city <u>expensive</u>?
   B: Yes, it's <u>really</u> expensive!

2. **A:** Do you like living in an <u>apartment</u>?
   B: No, I like living in a <u>house</u> much more.

3. **A:** Is your neighborhood <u>new</u> or <u>old</u>?
   B: The houses are very <u>old</u>.

4. **A:** Can you <u>walk</u> to school?
   B: No, I <u>can't</u>. It's too <u>far</u>.

Engage!

What are some new things in your city?

Are there any <u>parks</u> in your neighborhood?

Yes, there are <u>two</u>.

B 🔁 Read the exchanges in exercise **A** with a partner. Stress the underlined words.

C 🔁 Take turns asking and answering three questions about your neighborhood. Stress the important words.

Conversation

A 🔊 14 Close your book and listen to the conversation. What is the problem in Sarah's neighborhood?

Ben: How do you like living in your neighborhood?

Sarah: Well, it has a lot of beautiful old buildings, but there are some problems.

Ben: Like what?

Sarah: It doesn't have many different stores. There's only one supermarket, so food is very expensive.

Ben: That sounds like a pretty big problem.

Sarah: It is, but the city is building a new shopping center now. Next year, we'll have more stores.

B 🔁 Practice the conversation with a partner. Switch roles and practice it again.

C Write the words or phrases from the box in the correct column. Add two more ideas to each column.

Good things in a neighborhood	Bad things in a neighborhood

beautiful buildings
crime
a lot of noise
heavy traffic
public transportation
pollution
trees and green space
many different stores

D 🔁 Make two new conversations. Use your ideas from exercise **C**.

E 👥 What are the three most important things for a good neighborhood? Talk about your ideas in exercise **C**. Make a new list together. Give reasons.

Most important things for a good neighborhood	Reason
1.	
2.	
3.	

F 👥 **GOAL CHECK** ✔ **Explain what makes a good neighborhood**

Explain your group's list to the class.

Language Expansion: Using maps

A Study the map. Write the word from the box in the correct space.

| South |
| symbols |
| East |
| key |
| West |
| scale |

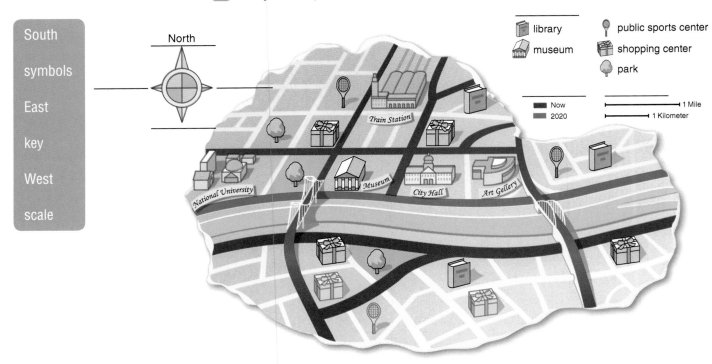

B 🔄 Take turns asking and answering the questions.

> **Where's the train station?**

> **It's in the north of the city.**

1. In which parts of the city are the libraries?

2. Where are the public sports centers?

3. Where will the new road be?

4. How many shopping centers does the city have now? How many do you think it will have in 2020?

5. What do you think this city needs?

Grammar: *Will* + time clauses

A Study the sentences and circle the correct letter.

I will finish my homework <u>before I go to bed</u>.

1. What will you do first?

   a. Finish my homework.   **b.** Go to bed.

2. The word *before* shows the action that happens . . . .

   a. first   **b.** second

I will wash the dishes <u>after I eat dinner</u>.

1. What will you do first?

   a. Wash the dishes.   **b.** Eat dinner.

2. The word *after* shows the action that happens . . . .

   a. first   **b.** second

I'll look at the neighborhood carefully **before I choose a new apartment.**
Before I choose a new apartment, I'll look at the neighborhood carefully.
I'll meet my neighbors **after I move into my new apartment.**
After I move into my new apartment, I'll meet my neighbors.

*A time clause tells when something happens. Use *before* or *after* at the beginning of a time clause.
*In a sentence with *will*, use the simple present tense in the time clause.
*The time clause can come first or second in the sentence. If the time clause is first, it is followed by a comma.

B Use the words below and the information in the note to make sentences with time clauses.

1. find a place for the meeting/make an invitation (after)

2. make a list of things to talk about/give invitations to all the neighbors (before)

3. make a list of things to talk about/have the meeting (before)

4. have the meeting/ask the city government for a sports center (after)

5. talk to newspaper reporters/ask the city government for a sports center (after)

May 2 find place for the meeting
May 3 make invitation
May 5–12 give invitations to neighbors
May 13 make list of things to talk about
May 25 have the meeting
May 26 ask city government for sports center
May 27 talk to newspaper reporters

Conversation

A Practice the conversation. What does Jennie want for her neighborhood?

Jennie: This neighborhood really needs a library.
Dan: You're absolutely right. But how can we get one?
Jennie: I think we should have a neighborhood meeting to talk about it.
Dan: That's a good idea. And after we have the meeting, we'll write a letter to the newspaper.
Jennie: Great! I'll help you.

B Make new conversations to talk about places in your neighborhood.

C GOAL CHECK ✔ **Discuss an action plan**

What does your city need? List things you can do to make your plan happen. Use time clauses to discuss when you will do each thing on the list. Then compare your list with a partner.

GOAL 4: Make Predictions About Cities in the Future

Reading

A  How did people get their food in the past, and what kinds of food did they eat? How is it different from our food today? How will it change in the future? Use the words below. Share your ideas with a partner.

produce	healthy food	grow
distribute	transport	

B Check (✓) the ideas that are in the reading.

_____ 1. Cities need safe and healthy food.

_____ 2. If we know how people in the past got food in cities, we can do the same things that they did.

_____ 3. City populations will triple by 2050.

_____ 4. In the future, we will need to change the way we grow food.

C Match the problems and the solutions from the reading.

_____ 1. It takes a lot of fossil fuel to produce food.

_____ 2. Our ways of producing food are not efficient.

_____ 3. We don't take care of the natural world.

a. We can study ways people got food in the past.

b. We can grow food more sustainably.

c. We can grow food closer to cities.

TED Ideas worth spreading

Carolyn Steel Architect, Food urbanist

HOW FOOD SHAPES OUR CITIES

How do you feed a city? It's an important question, but we rarely ask it. We take it for granted that we will find food in any restaurant or supermarket that we walk into. It's almost magic! Many of us don't think about **agriculture** at all. Many of us don't know who grew our food, who harvested it, or how it got from the farm to the city. But without good, healthy food, we—and our cities—won't survive.

Carolyn Steel is an architect who studies how ancient food routes shaped our modern cities. By understanding how city **dwellers** have gotten their food in the past, she thinks we can come up with better ways to produce and distribute food in the cities of the future.

By 2050, twice as many people will live in cities as do now. We will **consume** twice as much meat and **dairy** as we do today. This modern diet, heavy in meat, dairy, and processed food, requires enormous amounts of energy to produce. That energy mostly comes from fossil fuels, which are not renewable. We're also using fossil fuels to clear millions of acres of rainforest each year for planting crops and then to transport the crops to cities around the world. If we don't change the way that food is produced, we will have a serious problem. It will be very difficult to feed everyone.

How can we change our food systems so that we will be able to feed ourselves? Steel proposes producing food closer to our cities, as our ancestors did. Additionally, starting community agriculture programs in urban

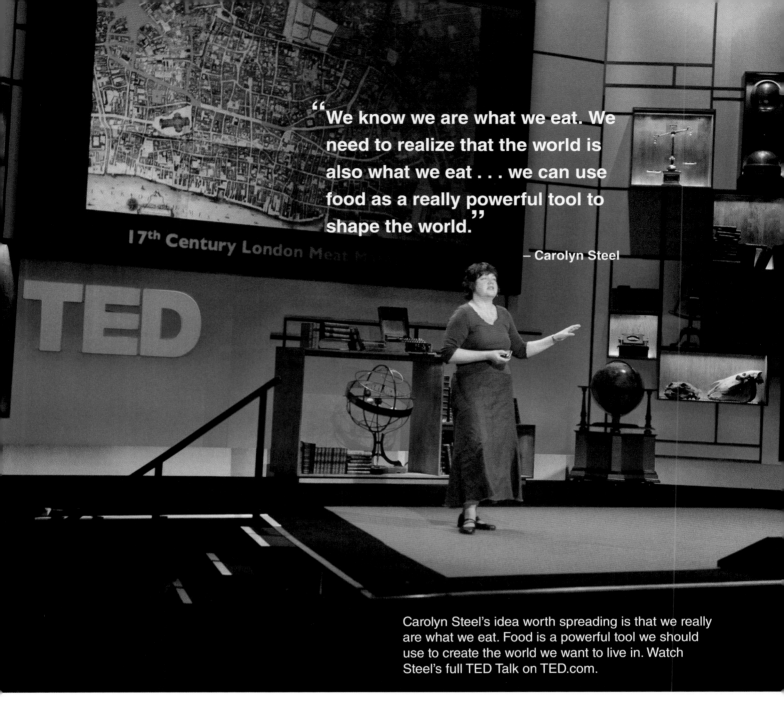

"We know we are what we eat. We need to realize that the world is also what we eat . . . we can use food as a really powerful tool to shape the world."

– Carolyn Steel

17th Century London Meat M

TED

Carolyn Steel's idea worth spreading is that we really are what we eat. Food is a powerful tool we should use to create the world we want to live in. Watch Steel's full TED Talk on TED.com.

areas will allow us to grow some of our own food. Steel believes that when we can see how our food is produced, and grow some of it ourselves, it will strengthen our connection with nature. And if we are connected to the natural world, we will **value** and protect it.

agriculture the science or occupation of farming
dweller a person or animal that lives in a particular place
consume to use (fuel, time, resources, etc.)
dairy milk and food made from milk (such as butter and cheese)
value to think that (someone or something) is important or useful

▲ Market in Madeira, Portugal

cold/moderate/hot	
climate	ocean
inland	hunting
fishing	immigrants
native people	

population	climate
transport	resources
traditions	environment
eating habits	

Communication

A Share your ideas of how food has shaped your city with a partner. Think about its location, its environment, and its culture. Use the words in the box.

Writing

A How will food in your city change in the future? Write six ideas and rank them in order of importance. Use the words in the box.

____ 1. _____   ____ 4. _____

____ 2. _____   ____ 5. _____

____ 3. _____   ____ 6. _____

B Complete the paragraph with *will* or *won't* and the verb in parentheses.

In the future, the population of cities (1) _____ (grow)

twice as big as it is now. We (2) _____ (be) able

to keep producing food the way we do in the present. People

(3) _____ (need) to grow food closer to where they live.

C Write a paragraph with predictions about cities in the future. Use *will* and words in the box to make your prediction.

D **GOAL CHECK** ✓ **Make predictions about cities in the future**

Work with a group. Share your paragraphs and support your opinions with facts. Which predictions are the most/least realistic?

Bouananiya Medersa
in Morocco

Before You Watch

A Read about the video and check the meanings of the words in **bold.**

While You Watch

A ▶ Watch the video. Write **T** for *true* or **F** for *false*.

_____ **1.** In the past, the Bouananiya Medersa was a palace.

_____ **2.** Restorers are taking old paint off the walls of the Medersa.

_____ **3.** The government isn't interested in restoring historic buildings in Fes.

_____ **4.** There is a problem because wealthy people want to live in the old houses in Fes.

B ▶ Watch the video again. Circle the correct answer.

1. The city of Fes was founded in the (ninth | eleventh) century.

2. By the 1300s, Fes was a center for (art | science) and learning.

3. (One or two | five or six) families live in each house in the medina.

4. In the future, the Medersa will be a (museum | school).

After You Watch / Communication

A What are some important buildings and places in your city's heritage? Make a list and then share the information with your partner.

B Write a guide for foreign visitors to a historic place in your city. Answer these questions in your guide.

1. What happened there? What can visitors see and do there?

2. How much does it cost to visit? What hours is it open? How can visitors get there?

The Bouananiya Medersa in Fes, Morocco, is a **masterpiece** of art. It's in very bad condition now, but people are working to **restore** its walls and **fountains.** Some old buildings in Fes are in danger because **wealthy** people buy and take away pieces of them. Now, **private** organizations are trying to **preserve** these buildings for the future. They hope all people can enjoy Morocco's **heritage.**

▲ Bouananiya Medersa in Fes, Morocco

TEDTALKS

Before You Watch

Charlie Todd's idea worth spreading is that play is a good thing—however old you are. Watch Todd's full TED Talk on TED.com.

Improv Everywhere is a group that creates

(1) _____ in public places. Their

founder, Charlie Todd, believes that

(2) _____ is as important for adults

as it is for kids. He was (3) _____

to start the group when he couldn't find a

regular theater to perform in. Now, Improv

Everywhere's (4) _____ members

can be found all around the world. So the next

time a group of people are (5) _____

on the street or a store, you might be seeing an

Improv Everywhere performance.

A 🔁 Look at the picture and answer the questions with a partner.

1. Where are these people?

2. What do people usually do here?

3. What are these people doing?

B Charlie Todd is a man who delights in creating unexpected scenes like the one in the picture above. Here are some words you will hear in his TED Talk. Complete the paragraph with the correct form of the word. Not all words will be used.

> **cop** *n.* a police officer
> **diverse** *adj.* made up of people or things that are different from each other
> **improvise** *v.* to speak or perform without preparation
> **inspire** *v.* to give (someone) an idea about what to do or create
> **play** *n.* activities that are done especially by children for fun or enjoyment
> **prank** *n.* a trick that is done to someone usually as a joke

C Look at the pictures on the next page. Check (✓) the information that you predict you will hear in the TED Talk.

____ **1.** We perform in many different public places.

____ **2.** Our goal is to make people smile and laugh.

____ **3.** Our performances are only for paying audiences.

While You Watch

A ▶ Watch the TED Talk. Circle the main idea.

1. Charlie Todd couldn't find work as an actor.

2. Everyone needs to be creative and have fun.

3. Improv Everywhere creates pranks that are positive experiences.

"There is no point and [. . .] there doesn't have to be a point. We don't need a reason. As long as it's fun."

– Charlie Todd

B ▶ Look at the photos. Watch the TED Talk again and write the letter of the caption under the correct photo.

a. Improv Everywhere's pranks take place in public places.

b. Nobody expects to see characters from a movie at the library.

c. Getting a high five on your way to work might make your day better.

d. Charlie Todd wants to share a sense of fun and play.

1. ___

2. ___

3. ___

4. _a_

Challenge! 🗨 Some people might object to Improv Everywhere's pranks. Why? Are Improv Everywhere's pranks a good idea or a bad idea? Tell a partner. Give examples to support your idea.

Charlie Todd Comedian, Founder of Improv Everywhere
THE SHARED EXPERIENCE
OF ABSURDITY

After You Watch

A Complete the summary with the words in the box.

Charlie Todd (1) _____ that we should be having more fun.

In 2005, he staged an Improv Everywhere prank when he asked a group of

friends to (2) _____ in the window frames of a building. Todd

calls their (3) _____ "missions," and the (4) _____

are "secret agents." Since the first prank, Todd and his group have

(5) _____ more than 100 missions and some of them have

become an international (6) _____.

> stand   actors
> believes   completed
> event   performances

B Match the phrases to the information from the TED Talk.

_____ **1.** number of high fives Rob gave   **a.** 2006

_____ **2.** number of agents participating in "Blue Shirt" mission   **b.** 8

_____ **3.** number of windows in the building   **c.** 80

_____ **4.** year he was insipired to do "Blue Shirt" mission   **d.** 2,000

_____ **5.** age of one young "secret agent"   **e.** 70

C Circle the statements that paraphrase Charlie Todd's ideas.

1. When I moved to New York, I wanted to be famous.

2. I started performing in public because I couldn't use a theater.

3. We want to create performances that make people happy.

4. Riding the subway in New York is a pleasant experience.

5. Adults need to learn to play again.

Project

Charlie Todd and his group Improv Everywhere are on a mission to make New Yorkers laugh. They play pranks in public places, creating shared, positive experiences. Use Todd's ideas to design an improvised performance in your own city.

A Look at the list of places Improv Everywhere "agents" have performed. Circle the ones you think would be the most fun.

> beach   park   public library   store   subway   car   train station

B Compare your choices in exercise **A** with a partner. Where else could you perform in your town or city? Remember that your goal is to create a positive, shared experience for the people who see your performance.

C Work with a group. Decide where you will perform and what activity you will do. Give each person in your group something specific to do. Use the table to organize your ideas.

Place	Date & Time	Activity	People

Challenge! Charlie Todd and Improv Everywhere really are everywhere—they even pulled a prank at TED. Go to TED.com and find out more about the prank they played. How did they do it?

The Body

A man doing a back flip off of a tree
stump in Mallorca Island, Spain

UNIT 4 GOALS

1. Discuss ways to stay healthy

2. Talk about lifestyles

3. Suggest helpful natural remedies

4. Explain cause and effect

brain

bone

artery

vein

heart

muscle

lungs

liver

stomach

small intestine

skin

large intestine

Vocabulary

A Look at the picture. Then fill in the blanks with the vocabulary words.

1. This pushes your blood through your body: _____

2. These carry blood around your body: _____ , _____

3. These bring air into your body: _____

4. This covers the outside of your body: _____

5. This makes your body move: _____

6. This lets you think and remember: _____

7. This does many different things: _____liver_____

8. These digest food: _____ , _____ , _____

9. This supports your body: _____

B 🔊 **15** Listen and check (✓) the words you hear.

☐ brain	☐ lungs	☐ liver
☐ large intestine	☐ vein	☐ muscle
☐ heart	☐ stomach	☐ small intestine
☐ artery	☐ bone	☐ skin

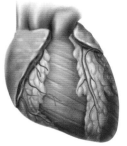

▲ human heart

▲ human fist

Grammar: The comparative, superlative, and equative

The comparative expresses similarities or differences between two people or things. Form the comparative with an adjective + -er + than or more/less + adjective + than.	The small intestine is **longer than** the large intestine. Henry is **healthier than** his father.
The superlative expresses extremes among three or more people or things. Form the superlative with the + adjective + -est or the most/least + adjective.	The skin is **the largest** organ in the human body. Some people think that the liver is **the most important** organ in the body.
The equative is used when people or things are the same or equal to each other. Form the equative with (not) as + adjective + as.	Your heart is **as large as** your fist. Your stomach is **not as large as** your liver.

Add -er/-est to most adjectives with 1 or 2 syllables. Use more/less or the most/least with adjectives of 3 or more syllables. When adjectives end in -y, change the -y to -i and add -er/-est.

Some adjectives have irregular comparative and superlative forms: good better best / bad worse worst / far farther farthest

A Complete the sentences. Use comparatives, superlatives, equatives, and the words in parentheses.

1. Walking for exercise is _____ (good) than running.
2. Smoking is the _____ (bad) thing you can do to your lungs.
3. Drinking alcohol is _____ (harmful) to your liver than eating junk food.
4. I think vegetables are the _____ (nutritious) kind of food for your brain.
5. Swimming is not the _____ (quick) way to build up your arm muscles.
6. Some elderly people are _____ (healthy) as some young people.

B Do you agree or disagree with the statements above? Use comparatives, superlatives, and equatives.

> I agree. Running is bad for your knees.

> But it's harder work, so maybe it's better for your heart.

Conversation

A (() 16 Close your book and listen to the conversation. Which body parts do the speakers mention?

Ron: What are you eating? It looks better than my lunch.
Valerie: It's fish stew, and it *is* good! Did you know that fish is good for your brain?
Ron: Really? Is it good for anything else?
Valerie: Well, it's also low in fat, so it's probably good for your arteries.
Ron: And it's high in protein, right? So it could help you build muscles.
Valerie: Yes, I think you're right.
Ron: My lunch isn't as good as yours. I just have a cheese sandwich.
Valerie: But cheese has a lot of calcium. That's good for your bones.
Ron: That's right! Enjoy your lunch.
Valerie: You, too.

B Practice the conversation with a partner. Then make a new conversation using foods you know about.

C GOAL CHECK ✔ **Discuss ways to stay healthy**

Talk with your partner about things you do to stay healthy. Complete these sentences:

I try to _____.

I try not to _____.

> I try to get some exercise every day.

> I try not to eat a lot of sugar.

Real Language

Common equative expressions include:

As soon as possible

As much as possible

Word Focus

genes = parts of a cell that control physical characteristics (eye color, height, etc.)

lifestyle = how we live

Listening

A 🔁 Discuss these questions with a partner.

1. What determines how healthy you are?

2. Are your **genes** or your **lifestyle** more important?

B 🔊 17 Listen to three people talk about their health. Match the speaker to the correct picture.

Speaker _____

Speaker _____

Speaker _____

C 🔊 17 Listen again and answer the questions.

Speaker A:

1. What kind of exercise does Speaker A get? _____

2. Which family members does Speaker A mention? _____

Speaker B:

3. What kind of exercise does Speaker B get? _____

4. How often does Speaker B get sick? _____

Speaker C:

5. Why did Speaker C change her diet when she got older? _____

6. What do some people think about Speaker C's diet? _____

D 🔁 Work with a partner. Interview each other. Then tell the class about your partner's lifestyle. Find out about:

• Exercise: What kind? How often?

• Diet: What do you usually eat?

• Genes: Do family members have health problems?

• Stress: How much and what kind?

Ask other questions about lifestyle that you think are important.

Pronunciation: Linking with comparatives and superlatives

> **Linking with comparatives and superlatives**
>
> When we use the comparative **-er** or **more,** and the next word starts with an /r/ sound, the words are linked together.
>
> When we use the superlative **-est** or **most,** and the next word starts with a /t/ sound, the words are linked together.
>
> **She'll run in a longer race next month.   We had the best time of our lives.**

A 🔊 **18** Listen to the sentences. Notice how the sounds are linked. Listen again and repeat the sentences.

1. It's a stricter religion than my religion.
2. This is the best tea for your stomach.
3. My grandfather is a faster runner than I am.
4. Which exercise is the most tiring?
5. You'll need a better reason than that.

B 🔁 Underline the sounds that link together. Then read the sentences aloud to a partner.

1. This is the longest text message I've ever seen.
2. Today's news was more reassuring than yesterday's news.
3. What's the best time of the day for you to study?
4. Flower experts are trying to develop a redder rose.
5. He took the softest towel in the house.

Communication

A 🔗 What are the best kinds of food and exercise for a healthy lifestyle? Rate the foods from least healthy (1) to healthiest (5). Add one idea of your own. Then do the same with the types of exercise. Compare your list with the list of another pair.

____ fruit ____ bread ____ meat ____ vegetables ____ _____

____ walking ____ running ____ swimming ____ yoga ____ _____

B 🔁 **GOAL CHECK** ✓ **Talk about lifestyles**

Talk to a partner. Who are the healthiest people you know? What are some reasons for their good health?

Engage!

Is your generation healthier or less healthy than your parents' generation?

> **I feel good if I eat some meat or fish every day.**

> **But is meat a healthier food than vegetables?**

Language Expansion: Everyday ailments

For every common health problem, there's a product for sale to cure it. Are you suffering from insomnia? There's a pill to help you fall asleep. Did a pimple appear on your face? There's a cream for that. If you have a headache after a long day at work, or perhaps a sore throat and fever, you can buy something to make you feel better. Do you have indigestion because you ate the wrong kind of food? There's a pill to end the burning feeling in your stomach. If food won't stay in your stomach at all, you can take some medicine to end the nausea. Or maybe you ate too fast, so now you have the hiccups. Well, you won't find anything at the pharmacy for hiccups, but there's probably a company working on a new product right now.

A Write the words in blue next to their definition.

1. _____ not being able to sleep

2. _____ high body temperature

3. _____ a repeated sound in your throat, often from eating too quickly

4. _____ a feeling like you are going to vomit

5. _____ pain in the stomach because of something one has eaten

6. _____ a small raised spot on the skin

7. _____ a pain in your head

8. _____ a general feeling of pain in the throat

B Read the article about natural remedies. What other natural remedies do you know about?

A Natural Solution

Garlic for a cold? Mint for bad breath? These days, more and more people are turning to their grandparents' remedies to cure their minor illnesses. And why not? These natural remedies are usually safe, inexpensive, and best of all—they work! (At least for some of the people, some of the time.) So the next time you're looking for a cure, skip the pharmacy and head to the grocery store for:

- **lemons** to stop the hiccups (Bite into a thick slice.)
- **ginger** to end nausea (Grind it and add hot water to make a tea.)
- **milk** to cure insomnia (Drink a warm glass at bedtime.)
- **honey** to help a sore throat (Mix it with warm water and drink it slowly.)
- **onions** to relieve a headache (Put slices on your forehead, close your eyes, and relax.)

garlic

lemon

olive oil

onion

ginger

> If my skin feels dry, I put some olive oil on it.

Grammar: Infinitive of purpose

The infinitive of purpose gives a reason for doing something. Form an infinitive with *to* + the simple or base form of a verb.	You can drink tea with honey **to help** a sore throat. I use a sunscreen **to protect** my skin.
In order to + the base form of a verb is also a way to express the infinitive of purpose.	Nikki took an aspirin **in order to lower** her fever.
Use a comma after the infinitive of purpose when it begins a sentence.	**To stop hiccups,** I drink a glass of water.

A Match the actions with the reasons.

1. Get plenty of sleep at night _____
2. Eat fruits and vegetables _____
3. Take a nap _____
4. Give children warm milk _____
5. Ask your doctor questions _____
6. Lift weights _____

a. to help them fall asleep.

b. to find out the best remedy for your problem.

c. to increase your concentration during the day.

d. to make your muscles stronger.

e. to get enough vitamins in your diet.

f. to cure a headache.

Conversation

A 🔊 **19** Close your book and listen to the conversation. What remedies for fatigue do the speakers talk about?

Olivia: Hi, Ashley. Are you drinking coffee? That's new.

Ashley: Hi, Olivia. You're right. I usually don't drink coffee, but I need it today to wake up.

Olivia: You do look tired. Did you get enough sleep last night?

Ashley: No, I was worried about today's test, so it was hard to fall asleep.

Olivia: Come on. Let's go for a walk.

Ashley: Go for a walk? Why?

Olivia: To wake you up and to get some oxygen to your brain before the test.

Ashley: That's a good idea. Where do you want to go?

B 🔁 Practice the conversation with a partner. Find and underline the three uses of the infinitive of purpose.

C 🔁 Make a new conversation using your own ideas about health problems. Then role-play the conversation for the class.

D 🔁 **GOAL CHECK** ✓ **Suggest helpful natural remedies**

Talk to a partner. What do you usually do to cure these common problems: a headache, bad breath, sore feet, and hiccups?

> **Real Language**
>
> We say *That's new* when we notice something different or unusual.

Reading

A 🔁 Talk to a partner. Which of these can make you sick?

- shaking hands with someone
- being outside in cold weather
- eating food
- riding a crowded bus
- touching your eye
- playing a computer game

B Circle **T** for *true* or **F** for *false*.

1. Viruses can only live inside people or animals. **T** **F**
2. All bacteria cause illnesses. **T** **F**
3. Washing your skin can prevent some illnesses. **T** **F**
4. Germs can enter the body through the eyes. **T** **F**
5. After they kill germs, antibodies stay in the body. **T** **F**
6. Vaccines kill germs in the body. **T** **F**

C 🔁 Tell a partner about the last time you got sick. How did you feel? What did you do to feel better?

Communication

A 👥 Work in a small group. Make a list of serious illnesses that people in different parts of the world can get. How do people get those illnesses?

Word Focus

sense = see, hear, feel, etc.
influenza = illness
cut = opening in the skin
immune system = the body's way of preventing illness
weak = not strong

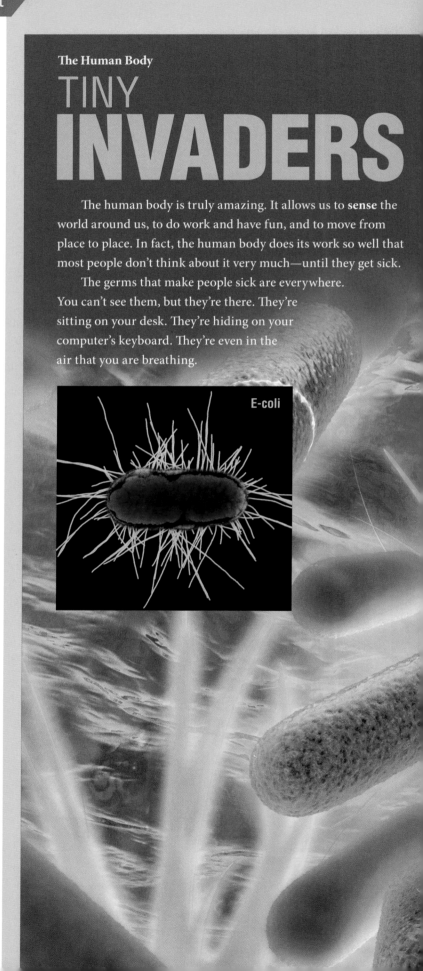

The Human Body

TINY INVADERS

The human body is truly amazing. It allows us to **sense** the world around us, to do work and have fun, and to move from place to place. In fact, the human body does its work so well that most people don't think about it very much—until they get sick.

The germs that make people sick are everywhere. You can't see them, but they're there. They're sitting on your desk. They're hiding on your computer's keyboard. They're even in the air that you are breathing.

E-coli

There are two types of germs: viruses and bacteria. Viruses use the cells inside animals or plants to live and multiply. Viruses cause illnesses such as **influenza,** or the flu. Bacteria are tiny creatures. Some bacteria are good. They can help your stomach digest food. Other bacteria aren't as good. They can cause sore throats and ear infections.

How can you stop these tiny invaders from making you sick? Your skin is the first defense against germs. One of the easiest ways to prevent some illnesses is simply by washing with soap and water. But germs can still enter the body through small **cuts** in the skin or through the mouth, eyes, and nose.

Once germs are inside your body, your **immune system** tries to protect you. It looks for and destroys germs. How does it do that? Some cells in the body actually eat germs! Other cells make antibodies. There is a different antibody for each kind of germ. Some antibodies keep germs from making you sick. Others help your body find and kill germs. After a germ is destroyed, the antibodies stay in your body. They protect you if the same kind of germ comes back. That way you will not get the same illness twice.

You can also help your immune system to fight germs by getting vaccinated. Vaccines are medicines. They contain dead or **weak** germs that cannot make you sick. Instead, they cause your body to make antibodies. If the same germ ever shows up again, then your antibodies attack it. You can also keep your body healthy by eating a healthy diet to make your immune system strong.

Legionella bacteria

Communication

A 👥 Talk with your classmates. How does each action on the left spread illness? Which actions on the right prevent illness?

> **Shaking a person's hand can pass on bacteria.**

> **Staying home will help prevent spreading germs.**

Ways to spread illness	Ways to prevent illness
shaking hands	Stay home when you're sick.
coughing or sneezing	Wash your hands often.
drinking from a friend's water bottle	Cover your nose and mouth.
sitting near a sick person at school	Use clean dishes for eating and drinking.
eating food without washing your hands	Exercise and eat healthy foods.

Writing

A Imagine your child is sick and cannot go to school today. Write a message to your child's teacher in your notebook. Explain how your child became ill and give reasons why you want him or her to stay at home.

_____
(date)

Dear (Mr./Ms.) _____ ,

_____

Sincerely,

_____

B 🗘 **GOAL CHECK** ✓ **Explain cause and effect**

Talk to a partner. What happens when viruses or bacteria enter the body?

Before You Watch

A 🔄 Brainstorm five things your body lets you do every day.

While You Watch

A ▶ Watch the video *The Human Body*. Draw lines to match the body's systems to the parts of the body or the cells they produce.

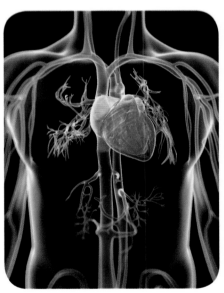

1. the circulatory system
2. the respiratory system
3. the digestive system
4. the nervous system
5. the reproductive system

a. the brain, spinal cord, and nerves
b. the heart
c. egg cells and sperm cells
d. the stomach and intestines
e. the lungs

B ▶ Watch the video again. Write **T** for *true* or **F** for *false*.

1. The heart is the body's strongest muscle. _____
2. Nutrients enter the blood from the small intestine. _____
3. The brain is about the size of an orange. _____
4. Another word for nerve cells is neurons. _____

After You Watch / Communication

A 🔄 What information from the video surprised you the most? What are some things you can do to take care of your body's systems?

B 🔗 Design a training program for an Olympic athlete. What will he or she eat every day? What kinds of exercise, and how often? What else will help to get your athlete into top physical condition?

Ford Ironman World Championship at
Kailua Bay in Kona, Hawaii

Look at the photo, answer the questions:

1 What phrase best describes the picture?

2 What do you think of when you hear the word *challenge*?

UNIT 5 GOALS

1. Talk about facing challenges

2. Discuss past accomplishments

3. Use *too* and *enough* to talk about abilities

4. Describe a personal challenge

▲ A young girl plays the stringed koto.

Word Focus

To face a challenge means to decide to do something new and difficult.

Word Focus

To **make progress** means to improve or get nearer to a goal over time.

Vocabulary

A 🔊 **20** Listen and read about one person's challenge.

The word "challenge" might make you think of physical activities like playing sports. But mental activities such as learning a new language or a new skill can also be a challenge. For me, learning to play a musical instrument is a challenge, but also an adventure. You might feel afraid to try it, but it's as exciting as traveling to a new place, and the only equipment you need is a violin, a guitar, or in my case—a *koto*.

When I started my *koto* lessons, my goal was to learn to play this amazing instrument well enough to play for my family. Now, I'm making good progress with the help of my music teacher. She thinks I'm getting better every week! I can probably achieve my goal soon, and then I'll play the *koto* at my father's birthday party.

B Write each word in blue next to the correct meaning.

1. related to the body _____

2. something new that requires effort _____

3. improvement _____

4. things needed for an activity _____

5. unusual and exciting activity _____

6. succeed in making something happen _____

7. related to the mind _____

8. something you hope to do over time _____

9. activity that requires special knowledge _____

10. surprising, interesting, and wonderful _____

Grammar: Past continuous vs. simple past

Past continuous vs. simple past	
Use the past continuous tense to talk about something in progress at a specific time in the past. Form the past continuous with *was/ were* + the *-ing* form of a verb.	I saw Sasha yesterday afternoon. He **was teaching** his son to ride a bicycle. We **weren't watching** a movie at 8:00 last night. We **were studying** for a test.
Use the simple past tense to talk about completed actions or situations in the past.	Edmund Hillary and Tenzing Norgay **climbed** Mount Everest in 1953.

Grammar: Past continuous with the simple past

Past continuous with the simple past	
Use the simple past with the past continuous to talk about a past event that interrupted something already in progress.	We **were practicing** the play **when** the lights **went** out.
Use a time clause with *when* for the action in the simple past and *while* for the action in the past continuous tense.	It **was raining** very hard **when they arrived** at the village. Sara **got** a text message **while she was talking** with her professor.
Use a comma after a time clause when it begins a sentence.	**While Ben was writing** his research paper, the computer stopped working.

A Complete the sentences. Use the past continuous form of the verb in parentheses.

1. William _____ (do) his homework when I arrived.

2. Martina _____ (look) for a job when I met her for the first time.

3. The mountain climbers _____ (rest) when the storm began.

4. While Ted and I _____ (wait) to see the doctor, I told him a funny story.

5. You and your friends _____ (sit) in the coffee shop yesterday morning.

Conversation

A ◀))） 21 Close your book and listen to the conversation. What was Helen's biggest challenge last year?

Helen: What was the most difficult thing you did last year?
Paul: Do you mean the worst thing?
Helen: No, I mean your biggest challenge.
Paul: Well, getting used to a new school when my family moved was a challenge.
Helen: For me, getting my driver's license was a challenge. It was hard!

B 🔁 Practice the conversation with a partner. What was difficult about each challenge?

C 🔁 **GOAL CHECK** ✔ **Talk about facing challenges**

Talk about a challenge you have faced with a partner. What was happening in your life at that time? How did the challenge change your life, or change you?

▲ Jenny Daltry, herpetologist and explorer

Listening

A What do you know about these endangered animals? Which animal do you think people should work the hardest to save? Why?

▲ giant panda

▲ Siamese crocodile

▲ Antiguan racer (snake)

▲ Humboldt penguin

B 🔊 **22**   Listen to the interview of Jenny Daltry. Circle the correct letter.

1. What amazing thing did Jenny Daltry do?

   a. She discovered a group of Siamese crocodiles.
   b. She found a new kind of bird in Cambodia.
   c. She helped scientists protect panda bears.

2. What was her biggest challenge?

   a. walking through marshes
   b. avoiding dangerous snakes
   c. educating people about crocodiles

3. How did she achieve her goal?

   a. She explained that crocodiles are important to the marshes.
   b. She explained that crocodiles are not really dangerous.
   c. She explained that crocodiles are extinct.

C 🔊 **22**   Listen again. Answer the questions.

1. How many crocodiles are in the largest group? _____

2. How many acres are now protected by the government? _____

3. How do most people feel about crocodiles? _____

   _____

4. What was Daltry doing when she found out about the Antiguan racer snake?

   _____

Pronunciation: Words that end in *-ed*

A 🔊 23 Listen to these words that end in *-ed*. The *-ed* is pronounced in three different ways.

/t/	/d/	/ɪd/
help helped	listen listened	start started

B 🔊 24 Listen, repeat, and check (✓) the column of the sound you hear.

Present tense	Simple past tense	-ed ending sound		
		/t/	/d/	/ɪd/
walk	walked	____	____	____
protect	protected	____	____	____
cross	crossed	____	____	____
discover	discovered	____	____	____
climb	climbed	____	____	____
start	started	____	____	____
need	needed	____	____	____
close	closed	____	____	____

C 📝 Write down ten verbs in the present tense. Some verbs should end in *t* or *d*. Say one of your words and ask your partner to say it in the past tense. Then switch roles.

Communication

A 📝 Work with a partner. Make a list of challenges people your age face.

B 👥 Get together with another pair of students and compare your lists. Try to agree on the two or three most difficult challenges for people your age.

C 📝 **GOAL CHECK** ✔ **Discuss past accomplishments**

Write two or three sentences about a famous person or a person you know. Choose from the list below or use your own idea. What challenges did he or she face in the past? How did the person achieve his or her goal? Tell your partner about the person you chose.

scientist or explorer   writer or artist   political figure   businessperson

---

Word Focus

To **achieve a goal** means to succeed in doing something you hoped to do.

▲ Subaru Takahashi, the youngest person to sail alone across the Pacific Ocean

Language Expansion: Phrasal verbs

A Read the article.

Subaru Takahashi was only 14 years old when he set out on an amazing adventure. His goal was to sail from Tokyo to San Francisco—alone. Subaru grew up near the sea and loved sailing. His parents thought he was old enough to sail alone, and they helped him buy a boat. He left on July 22. At first, the trip was easy. Then after three weeks, his engine broke down, so he didn't have any lights. He had to watch out for big ships at night, because it was too dark to see his boat. Five days later, his radio stopped working. Subaru was really alone then, but he didn't give up. His progress was very slow, but he kept on sailing. He almost ran out of food, and he was not fast enough to catch fish. He put up with hot sun and strong wind. On September 13, Subaru sailed into San Francisco. He was the youngest person ever to sail alone across the Pacific Ocean.

B Match each phrasal verb in blue from the article with its meaning.

1. set out _____	**a.** accept something bad without being upset
2. give up _____	**b.** grow from a child to an adult
3. watch out _____	**c.** finish the amount of something that you have
4. grow up_____	**d.** leave on a trip
5. keep on _____	**e.** be very careful
6. run out of _____	**f.** stop trying
7. put up with _____	**g.** continue trying
8. break down _____	**h.** stop working

Grammar: *Enough, not enough, too* + adjective

A Read these sentences from the article and the questions that follow. Circle **Y** for *yes* and **N** for *no*.

1. *He was <u>old enough</u> to sail alone.*
Could he sail alone? Y N

2. *He was <u>not fast enough</u> to catch fish.*
Did he catch fish? Y N

3. *It was <u>too dark</u> to see his boat.*
Could people see his boat? Y N

Enough, not enough, too + adjective	
He was **old enough** to sail alone.	adjective + *enough* = The amount that you want.
He was **not fast enough** to catch fish.	*not* + adjective + *enough* = Don't have the amount that you want.
His boat was **too dark** to see.	*too* + adjective = More than the amount you want.

B Complete the sentences. Use *enough, not enough*, or *too* and the adjective.

1. Subaru's boat was _____ (big) for two people.

2. A boat is _____ (expensive) for me to buy because I don't have much money.

3. Crossing the ocean alone is _____ (difficult) for most people to do.

4. My parents say I'm _____ (old) to travel alone. I have to wait until I'm 18.

5. I think Subaru's trip was _____ (dangerous) for a young person. His parents should not have let him go alone.

6. A trip to San Francisco by plane is a fun adventure, and it's _____ (safe) for my family and me. Maybe we'll go there for our next vacation.

Conversation

A 🔊 25 Close your book and listen to the conversation. What does Lisa need to do before she can climb the mountain?

Lisa: Do you know what I want to do next summer? My goal is to climb Black Mountain.

Mari: Are you serious? Black Mountain is too hard to climb. Don't you need special equipment?

Lisa: I already asked about it. I just need good boots.

Mari: And you're not strong enough to climb a mountain!

Lisa: You're right, I can't do it now. But I'll go hiking every weekend. Next summer, I'll be fit enough to climb the mountain.

Mari: Well, I like hiking. I'll go with you sometimes!

B 🔄 Practice the conversation with a partner. Then have new conversations about the activities in the box.

C 🔄 **GOAL CHECK** ✓ **Use *too* and *enough* to talk about abilities**

Write down six things you want to do. Discuss whether you can do these things now. Are you old enough to do them? Are they affordable or too expensive?

swim across a lake
travel to _____ (another country)
take a *karate* class

Reading

A What do you know about the Arctic? Circle the answers. Then read the article to check.

1. In the winter in the Arctic, it's dark _____ hours every day.

   a. 12   **b.** 20   **c.** 24

2. The North Pole is on _____.

   a. land   **b.** water   **c.** ice

3. In the Arctic, you can see _____.

   a. polar bears

   b. penguins

   c. polar bears and penguins

B Answer the questions in your notebook. If necessary, look back at the article.

1. What was Boerge and Mike's idea?

2. What happened to their food?

3. How did Boerge and Mike travel?

4. How far did they go every day?

5. What happened when they were close to the Pole?

6. When did they get to the Pole?

C Tell a partner about the expedition. In your opinion, what was the most amazing thing about the expedition?

Word Focus

float = to rest on top of water

tent = portable shelter

grab = to take suddenly

waterproof = does not allow water to get in

GPS = global positioning system

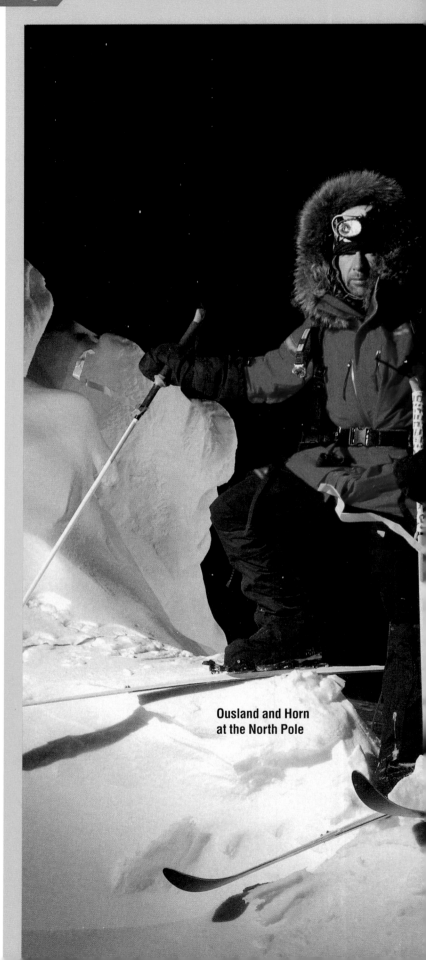

Ousland and Horn at the North Pole

ARCTIC DREAMS AND NIGHTMARES

Arctic Expedition

In the darkness of the Arctic night, a helicopter landed on the north coast of Russia. Boerge Ousland and Mike Horn were beginning one of the most amazing expeditions in history. It was January 22, and they planned to walk 600 miles (965 kilometers) to the North Pole—in winter.

There is no land at the North Pole, only water and ice that **floats** and moves. It's always a dangerous place, but winter is the worst time of the year. The sun doesn't come up for three months, and the temperature can be –40°F (–40°C). But Boerge grew up in Norway, and he loved skiing and climbing mountains. Mike Horn was a champion athlete from South Africa. They were ready for the challenge.

The two explorers wanted to set out right away, but the ice was moving too fast. They were waiting in their **tent** when Boerge heard a strange noise. "Mike, is that you?" Boerge asked. Suddenly, the tent ripped open. It was a polar bear! While they were looking for their guns, the bear **grabbed** some of their food. They didn't sleep very well that night.

The next day, they set out on skis and pulled their equipment behind them. When they came to open water, they had to swim. They put on **waterproof** suits over their clothes and got into the icy water five or six times a day. When they weren't in the water, they were skiing. It wasn't light enough to see, so they used headlamps.

Every day, they skied and swam north. And while they were sleeping, the ice carried them south. But they kept on for ten hours every day, covering 15 miles (24 kilometers) each day. They were making progress and getting close to the Pole when Mike became very ill. Blood was coming from his nose and ears. They had a cell phone, but Mike didn't want to give up and call for help. He took medicine, and he slowly got stronger. And every day, the sky got a little bit lighter.

On March 23, Boerge checked his **GPS.** The North Pole was 1000 yards (914 meters) away. "I've been there before," Boerge told Mike. "You've never been. You go first." "No," Mike said. "We'll do it together." And together, the two explorers walked to the Pole and took this amazing photo.

Communication

A 🔁 Discuss the questions with a partner.

1. People face challenges for different reasons, but there is usually some reward when we accomplish our goal. What are three or four challenges in life that cannot be avoided? (For example, it can be a challenge to get along well with all of our family members or neighbors.) What are the rewards if we face those challenges?

2. Tell your partner about two or three challenges in your life that you chose for yourself. Why did you choose to do those things?

Writing

A Write a paragraph about a challenging past experience from your own life in your notebook. Finish the topic sentence below. Then add interesting details. You may want to use time expressions such as "At first," "The next day," "After that."

Topic sentence: When I was _____ years old, I decided to _____

_____.

Details: It was a challenge because _____

_____.

B 🔁 **GOAL CHECK** ✔ **Describe a personal challenge**

Share your paragraph with a partner. Ask your partner questions about the information in the paragraph.

Snow Leopard running after prey

Before You Watch

A Fill in each blank with a word from the box. Use your dictionary to help you.

altitudes   camera shy
hunts   prey   trails

The snow leopard lives at high (1) ＿＿＿＿＿＿ in the mountains of Central Asia. There, the leopard (2) ＿＿＿＿＿＿ its (3) ＿＿＿＿＿＿: animals such as mountain goats and sheep. Snow leopards are (4) ＿＿＿＿＿＿ and few people have photographed them. For photographer Steve Winter, getting good pictures in these cold mountains was a physical and mental challenge. He and his team set up cameras on (5) ＿＿＿＿＿＿ where the leopards walk. Then they watched and waited.

While You Watch

A ▶ Watch the video. Check (✓) the activities in the box you see in the video.

B ▶ Watch the video again. Circle the best meaning for each word in **bold**.

1. Over the course of 10 months, photographer Steve Winter shot more than 30,000 **frames** in pursuit of the elusive snow leopard. (animals | pictures)

2. As few as 3,500 snow leopards may exist in the wild. They've been **spotted** as high as 18,000 feet, and they're notoriously camera shy. (seen | photographed)

3. Snow leopards can **leap** seven times their own body length. (walk | jump)

- ☐ driving on mountain roads
- ☐ cooking in a tent
- ☐ riding on horses
- ☐ fixing broken equipment
- ☐ touching a leopard
- ☐ setting up cameras

After You Watch / Communication

A 👥 Do you think Steve Winter got a lot of pictures of snow leopards? Why do you think Winter and his team decided to do such a difficult project?

Transitions

Kosavar Bosnian bride preparing for
traditional wedding in Donje Ljubinje
located in the Shar Mountains between
Kosovo and Macedonia

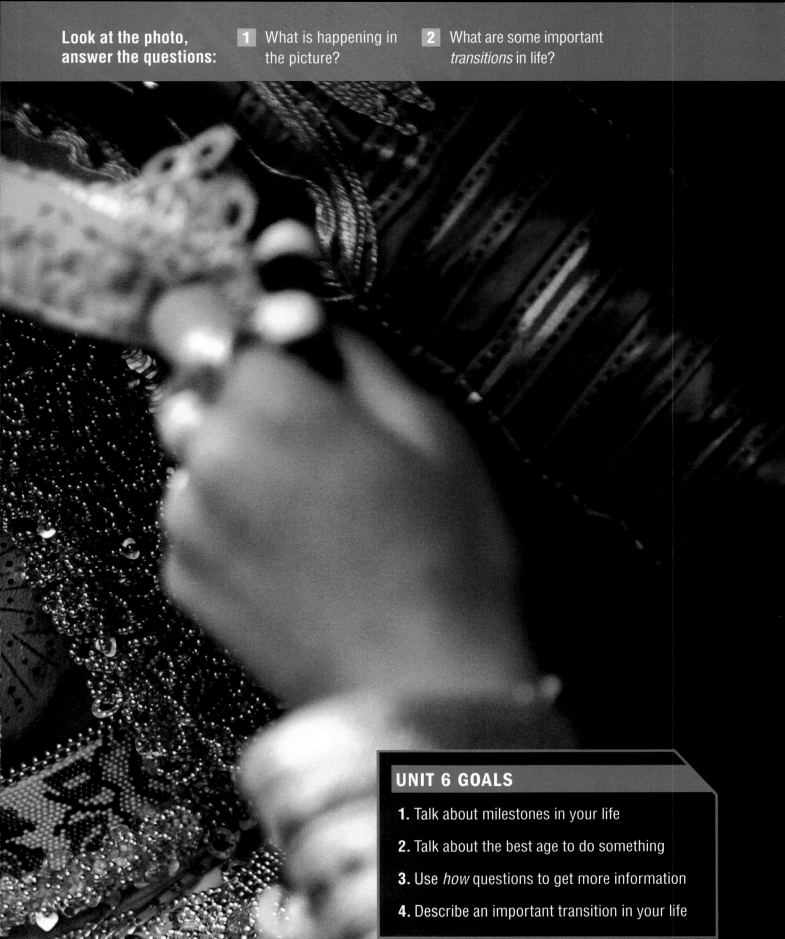

UNIT 6 GOALS

1. Talk about milestones in your life

2. Talk about the best age to do something

3. Use *how* questions to get more information

4. Describe an important transition in your life

an adult	a baby
a senior citizen	
a teenager	a child

▲ Infancy

He's _____ .

▲ Childhood

She's _____ .

A baby can't walk or talk. A child . . .

Vocabulary

A Complete the photo captions with a phrase from the box.

▲ Adolescence

He's _____ .

▲ Adulthood

She's _____ .

▲ Old Age

He's _____ .

B What do you think? At what age do people make these transitions?

1. from infancy to childhood _____
2. from childhood to adolescence _____
3. from adolescence to adulthood _____
4. from adulthood to old age _____

C Compare your answers in exercise **B** with a partner's answers. What changes take place in these transitions?

Grammar: Using the present perfect tense

Present perfect tense	
Use the present perfect to talk about actions which: 1. began in the past and continue until the present. 2. happened at an indefinite past time and which have an impact on the present. 3. happened repeatedly in the past.	1. He **has loved** music since he was a baby. (He still loves music now.) 2. Tim **has traveled** alone before, so he's not nervous about his trip to India. 3. Ken and Takako **have moved** three times.
Use the simple past for completed action or situation at a specific past time.	~~We have bought our house in 2011.~~ We bought our house in 2011.
The signal words *ever*, *never*, *already*, and *yet* are often used with the present perfect.	**Has** Justin **graduated** *already*? No, he **hasn't graduated** *yet*.

<table>
<tr><td>Use the present perfect with *for* to talk about how long something has been true.

Use the present perfect with *since* to talk about when a situation began.</td><td>Simone **has had** gray hair *for* ten years.
(That's how long.)

She **has known** her best friend *since* 2004.
(That's when they met.)</td></tr>
</table>

▲ City of Los Angeles, U.S.A

A Complete the sentences. Use the present perfect or simple past.

1. I _____ (live) in this apartment for five years. Before that,

   I _____ (live) with my parents.

2. Leonard _____ (graduated) from high school two years

   ago. He _____ (not, graduate) from the university yet.

3. Nora _____ (be, not) to South America, but she

   _____ (travel) in Mexico last year.

4. We _____ (start) this course two months ago.

   So far, we _____ (finish) five units.

B Which of these things have you done? When did you do them? Write sentences with the present perfect or simple past tense in your notebook.

1. vote
2. get married
3. move out of your parents' house
4. find a gray hair on your head

C Compare your answers in exercise **B** with a partner's answers. At what stage of life do people usually do these things? At what age?

Conversation

A 🔊 26 Close your book and listen to the conversation. Where did Jason go?

Rick: Have you ever traveled alone?
Jason: Yes, I have. It was fun!
Rick: Really? Where did you go?
Jason: I went to Los Angeles for a week last summer.
Rick: Did you stay in a hotel?
Jason: No, I visited my cousins. We had a great time.

B Practice the conversation with a partner. Then make a new conversation about your travel experiences.

C **GOAL CHECK** ✔ **Talk about milestones in your life**

Look at the stages of life on page 68. Write a question about a milestone (very important event) for each stage. Ask a partner your questions.

> **Where were you born?**

> **How long have you known your best friend?**

▲ Portrait of a 104 year old Okinawan woman

Listening

A 🔁 Discuss these questions with a partner.

1. Who is the oldest person you know? How old is he or she?

2. What does this person usually do every day?

B 🔊 **27** Listen to a radio program about Ushi Okushima, a woman from Okinawa, Japan. Answer the questions.

1. Where does Ushi work? _____

2. Why is Ushi unusual? _____

C 🔊 **27** Listen again and find the information needed below.

1. More than 700 people in Okinawa _____ .

2. Three reasons for this:

   a. _____
   b. _____
   c. _____

3. Ushi's advice:

   a. _____
   b. _____
   c. _____

D 🔁 Would you like to live to be 100? Discuss the question with a partner. Explain your reasons.

Pronunciation: The schwa sound /ə/ in unstressed syllables

A 🔊 **28** Listen to the words. Notice the vowel sound of the unstressed syllables in blue. This is the schwa sound /ə/, and it's the most common vowel sound in English.

infant   lettuce   children   population   adult

B 🔊 **29** Listen and repeat the words. Circle the unstressed syllables with the /ə/ sound.

alone	lesson	person	banana	parents
paper	challenge	language	national	chicken

Conversation

A 🔊 **30** Close your book and listen to the conversation. How old is Jamal?

Andrea:	Did you hear the big news? Jamal is getting his own apartment!
Kim:	Seriously? But he's 19! That's too young to get your own place.
Andrea:	Oh, I don't know about that.
Kim:	Do you think he's old enough?
Andrea:	Well, he's mature, and he's had a part-time job since he was 17.
Kim:	That's true . . . but I think he should wait a few years.
Andrea:	Really? What do you think is the best age to live on your own?
Kim:	I think people should get their own place after they've finished college.
Andrea:	That's a good point. I plan to live with my parents while I'm in college.

B 🔁 Practice the conversation with a partner. Switch roles and practice it again.

C 🔁 Make a chart with a partner in your notebooks. Use your own ideas. Then make new conversations about Jorge and Melissa using the conversation in exercise **A** as an example.

"Jorge is too old to change jobs."	"Melissa is too young to get her own apartment."
Age: _____	Age: _____
Reasons why it is or isn't OK	Reasons why it is or isn't OK
_____	_____
_____	_____
The best age for this is _____ .	The best age for this is _____ .

D Read the opinions. How old do you think each person is?

1. "He's too old to play soccer."   Age: _____

2. "He's too young to travel alone."   Age: _____

3. "She's too old to dance."   Age: _____

4. "She's too young to drive a car."   Age: _____

5. "She's too old to learn a new language."   Age: _____

6. "He's too old to get married."   Age: _____

E 🔁 **GOAL CHECK** ✓ **Talk about the best age to do something**

Look at your answers for **D**. Compare your answers with a partner and explain your opinions. What is the best age for each of these things? Do you know someone who does these things at an unusual age?

Language Expansion: Adjectives for age

A 🔄 Do you know someone who fits any of these descriptions? Who is it? Share your answers with a partner. Use the adjectives in the box to help you.

youthful	older, but with the energy of a young person (good)
childish	older, but acting like a child (bad)
elderly	looking and acting old
mature	old enough to be responsible and make good decisions
middle-aged	not young or old (about 40–60)
in his/her twenties	between 20 and 29 (also in his *teens, thirties, forties*, etc.)
retired	stopped working full-time (often after 65)

B 🔄 Talk about these people with a partner. How old are they? Describe them with adjectives from the box.

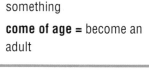

> I think she's in her teens, but she looks very mature.

Grammar: *How* + adjective or adverb

***How* + adjective or adverb**	
Adjectives give information about nouns. Use *How* + adjective to ask a question about a descriptive adjective.	Lenora is very **mature**. **How mature** is she? She's mature enough to babysit my son.
Adverbs give information about verbs. Use *How* + adverb to ask a question about an adverb.	I **learn quickly**. **How quickly** do you learn? I learned to ride a bicycle in one day!

A 🔄 Unscramble the questions. Take turns with a partner asking the questions.

1. English how do speak well you ___How well do you speak English___ ?

2. you how are old _____ ?

3. can fast you how type _____ ?

4. you how tall are _____ ?

5. your family how often move does _____ ?

B Complete the conversations. Write questions using *how*.

1. **A:** I think Mr. Chen is too elderly to live alone.
   B: He doesn't look old to me. _____ ?

2. **A:** My brother failed his driver's license test six times because he drives so badly.
   B: Wow! _____ ?

3. **A:** I can't go to the movie with you tonight, because my first class is very early tomorrow.
   B: That's too bad. _____ ?

4. **A:** I don't want to get my own apartment. It's much too expensive.
   B: Really? _____ ?

5. **A:** I haven't finished reading the assignment for tomorrow. I guess I read too slowly.
   B: That's a problem. _____ ?

Conversation

A 🔊 **31** Close your book and listen to the conversation. What did Erik get?

Mrs. Ryan: My son Erik just got his first credit card.
Mrs. Chen: He's still a university student.
Mrs. Ryan: That's true, but he has always been careful with money.
Mrs. Chen: Really? How careful is he?
Mrs. Ryan: He's very careful. In high school he saved enough money to buy a computer.
Mrs. Chen: Then maybe he is ready to get a credit card.

B 🔄 Practice the conversation with a partner. Switch roles and practice again.

C 🔄 Complete the descriptions on the right. Then make new conversations.

D 🔄 **GOAL CHECK** ✔ **Use *how* questions to get more information**

Take turns with a partner giving a description of yourself or how you do something. Ask questions with *how* to get as much information as possible.

Elizabeth, in her 60s

- started on a trip around the world
- independent

reasons: _____

_____

_____

_____

Keisha, 19

- got her own apartment
- mature

reasons: _____

_____

_____

_____

_____

Reading

A 🔁 Check (✓) the items below that show a transition in life. Share your ideas with a partner.

_____ **1.** get a new job

_____ **2.** go shopping

_____ **3.** buy a car

_____ **4.** begin college or university

_____ **5.** play soccer

_____ **6.** get married

B Read the text. Circle the correct option.

1. Amy Purdy is a champion (cyclist | snowboarder).

2. She has prosthetic (arms | legs).

3. Purdy (imagined | remembered) her new life.

4. Purdy's (book | organization) is called "Adaptive Action Sports."

C Write _True_ or _False_ next to the statements.

_____ **1.** Amy Purdy nearly died when she was 19.

_____ **2.** It wasn't difficult for her to recover from her illness.

_____ **3.** During her recovery, Purdy decided to control her life again.

_____ **4.** She helps other people by sharing her story with them.

_____ **5.** Purdy worked as a model before her illness.

D 🔁 How do you think _you_ would react in Purdy's situation? Share your ideas.

Amy Purdy Professional Snowboarder

LIVING BEYOND LIMITS

Amy Purdy is a world champion snowboarder who has won two World Cup competitions. She is an actress and model. She is also a double-**amputee.**

When Purdy was 19 years old, she became ill with a rare and serious form of meningitis. It almost killed her, and even though she survived the disease, she lost her kidneys, her spleen, the hearing in her left ear, and both of her legs below her knees. Purdy says that when she finally left the hospital, she felt like she "had been pieced back together like a **patchwork** doll." She received **prosthetic** legs, but they were clumsy and heavy. At first, it was hard for her to imagine how she would learn to walk again, and even harder to imagine that one day she would be able to fly down mountains on her snowboard and travel around the world.

Purdy spent months in bed. She struggled to recover from her illness, but she felt both physically and mentally broken. Finally, she realized that she had to make a change. She says, "I knew that in order to move forward I had to let go of the old Amy and learn to **embrace** the new Amy."

Even though she still faced many struggles, Purdy took charge of her life. "It was this moment that I asked myself that life-defining question: If my life were a book and I were the author, how would I want this story to go? And I began to daydream. I daydreamed like I did as a little girl. And I imagined myself walking gracefully, helping other people through my journey, and snowboarding again," she says.

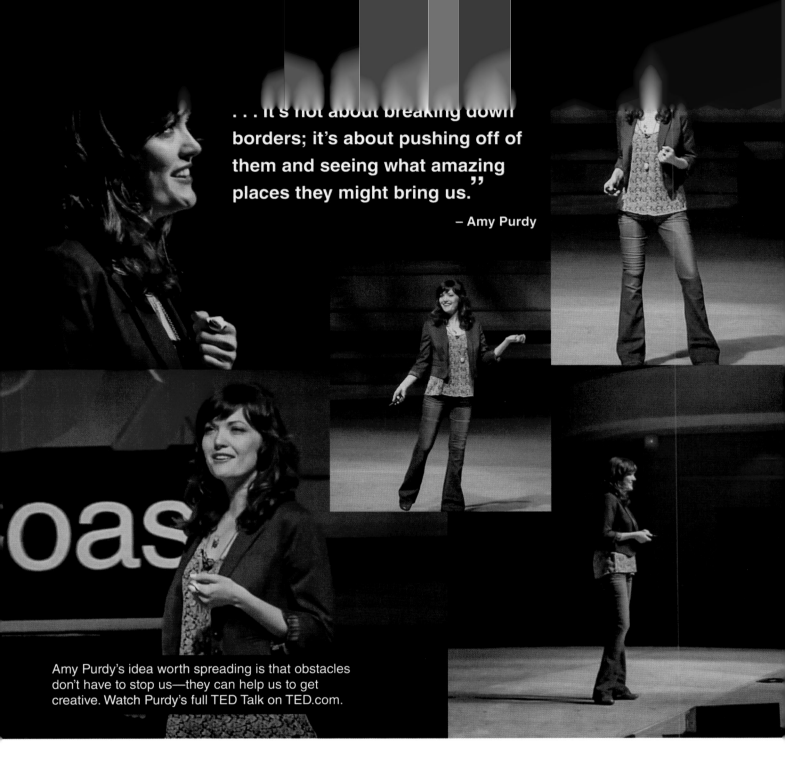

> ". . . It's not about breaking down borders; it's about pushing off of them and seeing what amazing places they might bring us."
>
> – Amy Purdy

Amy Purdy's idea worth spreading is that obstacles don't have to stop us—they can help us to get creative. Watch Purdy's full TED Talk on TED.com.

Since then, Purdy has done amazing things. She has acted in music videos and movies, earned a world ranking as a snowboarder, and traveled around the world. In 2005, she founded a **non-profit** organization called "Adaptive Action Sports" to help people with physical disabilities get involved in action sports. And most importantly, she has shared her story of inspiration and imagination, encouraging us all to live beyond our limits.

amputee *a person who has had an arm or a leg removed by surgery*
patchwork *pieces of cloth that are sewn in a pattern*
prosthetic *an artificial device that replaces a missing part of the body*
embrace *to accept readily or gladly*
non-profit *not done for money*

After becoming disabled, Amy Purdy imagined—and now lives—a very full life.

Communication

A Think about an important transition that you made in your life. What caused it? What effects did it have? Share your ideas with a partner.

Writing

A Circle the correct phrasal verbs in the sentences.

1. If you want to make a change in your life, you need to (take charge of | get over) it.

2. Transitions can be difficult, but if you (keep on | grow up) trying, you'll succeed.

3. Learning to snowboard was so challenging that Purdy nearly (set out | gave up).

B Write a paragraph in your notebook describing an important transition in your life. Include phrasal verbs in your writing.

When I was _____ years old, _____ _____. This transition was important to me because _____.

C **GOAL CHECK** ✓ **Describe an important transition in your life**

Share your ideas about transitions. What are some positive/negative reasons for making transitions?

Nubian women sing traditional songs as they arrive with gifts at the home of a newly-wedded bride

Before You Watch

A 🔁 Talk with a partner about weddings that each of you has seen. Use the topics and the question in the box to help you.

> the bride   the groom
> the party   the ceremony
> How were the two weddings similar or different?

While You Watch

A ▶ Watch the video. Number the parts of the wedding in order.

_____ Everyone eats a special dinner.

___1___ The bride and groom sign special legal papers.

_____ The groom puts a ring on the bride's finger.

_____ The bride's skin is painted.

_____ The groom leaves his parents' house.

B ▶ Watch the video again. Answer the questions.

1. When did Sheriff meet Abir? _____

2. How many days does the wedding last? _____

3. When does the party start each day? _____

4. When did life change for the Nubians? _____

5. What do people eat at the wedding? _____

6. Who kisses the groom? _____

After You Watch / Communication

A 🔁 What surprised you the most about the Nubian wedding? How is it similar to or different from weddings in your country?

Hans Rosling Professor of Global Health,
Co-founder Gapminder.org

THE MAGIC WASHING MACHINE

Before You Watch

A 🔁 Look at the picture and answer the questions with a partner.

1. What is this device? Do you have one in your house?

2. What percent of people have a modern washing machine?

3. How has it changed people's lives?

B Here are words you will hear in the TED Talk. Complete the paragraph with the correct words. Not all words will be used.

> **electricity** *n.* flow of energy used as power
> **heat** *v.* to cause (something) to become warm or hot
> **load** *v.* to put (an amount of something) into or onto something
> **mesmerize** *v.* to hold the attention of (someone) entirely
> **time-consuming** *adj.* using or needing a large amount of time
> **tough** *adj.* very difficult to do or deal with

It's amazing how machines can change the world. Not so many years ago, doing laundry was a (1) _____ job. You needed to (2) _____ the water, add the soap and the clothes, and rub them with your hands for a long, long time. Now, we (3) _____ the washing machine, push the button, and the machine does the rest. It's not (4) _____ to get your clothes clean at all. Of course, a washing machine uses (5) _____ to run, and this is a problem as more people get them.

> Hans Rosling's idea worth spreading is that machines have had an incredible effect on the lives of many—and rich westerners can't just tell those in the developing world that they can't have them. Watch Rosling's full TED Talk on TED.com.

C Look at the pictures on the next page. Check (✓) the information that you predict you will hear in the TED Talk.

_____ 1. Doing laundry is usually work for women and girls.

_____ 2. People in rich countries have a lot of different machines in their homes.

_____ 3. We should drive less and walk or ride bikes more.

While You Watch

A ▶ Watch the TED Talk. Circle the main idea.

1. Washing machines are very popular around the world.

2. Women like to read more than they like to do laundry.

3. When people don't have to do so much hard work, they have time to do things they enjoy and their lives change in positive ways.

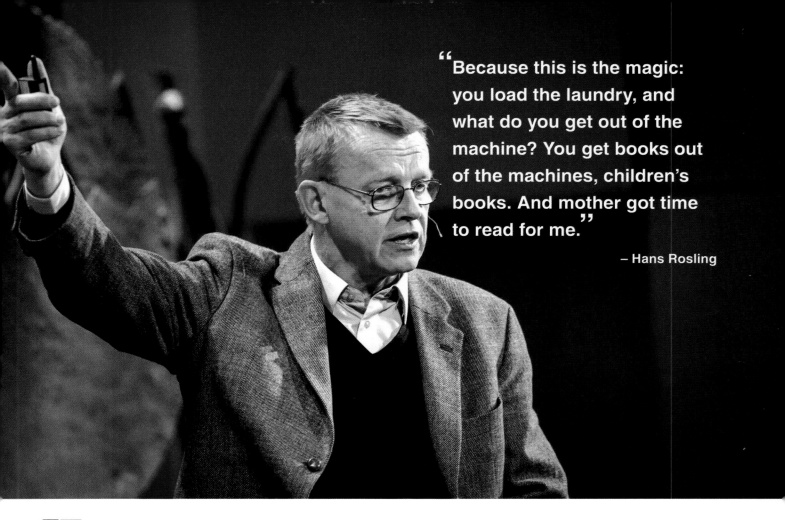

> "Because this is the magic: you load the laundry, and what do you get out of the machine? You get books out of the machines, children's books. And mother got time to read for me."
>
> – Hans Rosling

B ▶ The images below relate to the TED Talk. Watch the TED Talk again and write the letter of the caption under the correct photo.

a. Women in Sweden used to wash clothes by hand.

b. People in developed countries use half of the world's energy.

c. Having a washing machine gave Rosling's mother time to read.

1. ___

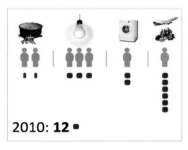

2010: **12** ●

2. ___

3. ___

Challenge! 🔀 What would happen if all families around the world could use a modern washing machine? What would be the benefits and the challenges? What does Rosling think we should do about the challenges? Share your ideas with the class. Give reasons for your opinions.

After You Watch

A Complete the summary with the words in the box.

| developing | education | improves | researches | washing |

Hans Rosling (1) _____ how people live around the world. He believes that by reducing hard work, like (2) _____ clothes by hand, women and girls in (3) _____ countries will have more time to read and study. Why is that important? Because when people have an (4) _____, their quality of life (5) _____.

B Match the phrases to state information from the TED Talk.

_____ **1.** number of people in the world   **a.** 22%

_____ **2.** amount the richest people spend daily   **b.** $2

_____ **3.** current total energy consumption   **c.** 7 billion

_____ **4.** amount the poorest people spend daily   **d.** $80

_____ **5.** future total energy consumption   **e.** 12%

C Read the statements below. Circle the ones that paraphrase Hans Rosling's opinions.

1. People in rich countries use much of the energy in the world.

2. Most people in the world are not very poor.

3. People who use a lot of energy shouldn't tell other people not to.

4. Getting a washing machine made a big difference in his family's life.

5. We should not have more technology in the world.

Project

Hans Rosling believes that small transitions in individual lives can make a big difference in the world. As people move out of poverty and do less time-consuming work, they gain time to get an education and find better jobs. Use his ideas to survey your classmates about an important transition for people in your country.

In many developing countries, women do the hard work of carrying water.

A Look at the list of devices. Circle the two you think have made the biggest difference in people's lives in the last century.

> microwave oven   vacuum cleaner   air conditioner
> computer   cell phone   dishwasher

B Compare your choices in exercise **A** with a partner. Are there any devices you'd like to add to the list? Think about devices that save on work and give people more time to read and get an education.

C Take a survey. Write a question for each item. Ask each question and then ask a follow-up question for details. Use the chart to take notes.

	Question	Name	Details
1. most expensive			
2. most useful at home			
3. helped the most people			
4. caused the biggest problems			
5. caused the most pollution			

> What's the most important device in the 21st century?

> I think it's the cell phone.

> Why do you think that?

Presentation Strategy

Using numbers to support facts

Hans Rosling uses numbers and statistics to surprise the audience and support his argument in interesting and humorous ways.

Challenge! Hans Rosling is interested in the differences between what we *think* we know about the world and the way things really are. He's also very curious about the ways the world is going to change. Go to TED.com and find another TED Talk by Hans Rosling. What has he learned, and what predictions does he make?

Luxuries

Baroque dinning room for Carnival party
in Venice, Italy

UNIT 7 GOALS

1. Explain how we get luxury items

2. Talk about needs and wants

3. Discuss what makes people's lives better

4. Evaluate the effect of advertising

Vocabulary

▲ handmade jewelry

_____

_____

▲ precious metals

_____

_____

▲ luxury clothing

_____

_____

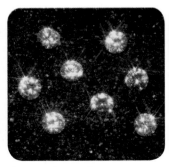

▲ precious stones

_____

_____

| pearl necklace   silver |
| diamonds   fur coat |
| emeralds   silk shirt |
| gold   expensive watch |

A Write each word or phrase from the box in the correct category above.

B Write three things your country imports and three things your country exports in your notebook. Share your lists with the class.

My country **imports** (buys from other countries)	My country **exports** (sells to other countries)

Grammar: Passive voice (present tense)

Notice

*Sometimes we use a *by* phrase with the passive voice.

Active voice	Passive voice
Subject + transitive verb + direct object	Direct object + *be* + past participle of transitive verb
Some people give jewelry as a gift. My country imports cars from Germany.	Jewelry **is given** as a gift (by some people). Cars are imported from Germany (by my country).
*Transitive verbs have direct objects. *Use the passive voice with transitive verbs when the focus is on the object.	*The object goes before the verb in the passive voice. *The passive voice is formed with the verb *be* plus the past participle of the main verb.

A Complete the sentences in the paragraph with the passive form of the verbs in parentheses.

Luxury items are expensive for a reason. Expensive watches, for example, _____ (make) from precious metals such as silver or platinum.

Beautiful jewelry _____ (produce) by people, not by machines.

Precious stones such as diamonds and opals _____ (separate) from

tons of rock, and that requires expensive machinery. Imported luxury items

_____ (bring) in from distant countries, so the cost of transportation

adds to their expense. Finally, a luxury item such as perfume _____

(make) from special ingredients that can only be found in a few places in the world.

Word Focus

mined = removed from under the Earth's surface

B Match the luxury items to the actions.

1. Pearls _____   **a.** are mined in several countries.

2. Animal skins _____ **b.** is exported from East Asian countries.

3. Silk _____   **c.** is sold in bottles.

4. Diamonds _____   **d.** are found inside oysters.

5. Perfume _____   **e.** are used to make fur coats.

C Take turns. Tell a partner about a luxury item you have or want to have. Where do you get it? How do you get it? How is it made?

Conversation

A 2 Close your book and listen to the conversation. Who made Ellen's blouse?

Sandra: That's a beautiful blouse! Is it silk?

Ellen: No, it's cotton, but it is soft like silk.

Sandra: I heard that the best cotton is grown in Egypt.

Ellen: Really? A lot of cotton is grown in India, too, but I don't know which kind is better.

Sandra: Where was your blouse made?

Ellen: In Sri Lanka. It was made by women in a co-op. They work together to make clothes. Then they are sold directly to the stores, and the women keep the profit.

Sandra: That's great!

B Practice the conversation with a partner. Switch roles and practice it again.

C **GOAL CHECK** ✓ **Explain how we get luxury items**

What luxury items are popular in your country? If the items are imported, where are they made? What are they made from? Who makes them? Tell a partner.

▲ Bouquets of roses for sale at a flower market

▲ a greenhouse

Listening

A 🔊 **3** Listen to three people talk about the cut-flower industry. Why is each country important to the flower industry?

1. Japan _____	**a.** has a good climate for growing flowers.
2. Ecuador _____	**b.** imports many flowers.
3. The Netherlands _____	**c.** develops new kinds of flowers.

B 🔊 **3** Listen again. Why is the flower industry important to each person?

1. Shinobu: _____

2. Rafael: _____

3. Peter: _____

Pronunciation: Content vs. function words

In sentences, content words have specific meaning and receive greater stress. Other words have a grammatical function and receive less stress.

Content words				
nouns	**main verbs**	**question words**	**adjectives**	**adverbs**
money	speak	why, where, how	wonderful	easily
Function words				
pronouns	**auxiliary verbs**	**the verb *be***	**articles**	**prepositions**
it, she, him	have, is, will, could	is, are, was	the, a/n	in, to, of, at

More function words
conjunctions
and, or, but, so

A 🔊 4 Listen to the stress in each sentence. Then listen again and repeat.

1. She <u>wants</u> to <u>go</u> to a <u>private</u> <u>college</u>.

2. We <u>have</u> to <u>pay</u> the <u>electric</u> <u>bill</u>.

3. The <u>bill</u> can be <u>paid</u> <u>online</u>.

4. My <u>family</u> <u>needs</u> the <u>money</u> I <u>make</u>.

5. I'm <u>saving</u> <u>money</u> for a <u>new</u> <u>computer</u>.

6. He <u>wants</u> a <u>Lexus</u>, but he should <u>buy</u> a <u>Toyota</u>.

B 🗘 Underline the content words. Then practice saying the sentences with a partner.

1. Flowers are an important part of life.

2. Delicious grapes can be grown in California.

3. I like diamonds and rubies, but they're very expensive.

4. My future could be very bright.

5. Celia wants to buy a new car.

6. Do you think she should get a small car?

Communication

A Write each item in the appropriate column. Use your own opinion.

a computer   a car   furniture   shoes   clean water   fresh fruit
books   flowers   money   a telephone   public parks   the Internet

Luxuries	Necessities

> **Word Focus**
>
> **Necessities** are things we need, such as food and shelter.
>
> **Luxuries** are things we don't really need, but they can be nice to have.

B 🗘 Compare your chart from exercise **A** with a partner's chart. Talk about why you think people need (or don't need) the items.

C 🗘 **GOAL CHECK** ✓ **Talk about needs and wants**

What is something you absolutely need? What luxury item do you want very much? Discuss these questions with a partner.

Persian rugs are still made by hand in parts of Iran.

Language Expansion

lose – lost   find – found
send – sent   give – given
put – put   freeze – frozen
build – built
know – known

A Fill in the blanks with the words in the box. Use your dictionary to help you.

1. Many kinds of precious stones can be _____ in Brazil.

2. Fresh seafood can be _____ by plane to anywhere in the world.

3. The seafood is _____ so that it stays cold until it arrives.

4. Iran is _____ for its beautiful handmade rugs.

5. Smartphones are _____ every day when they fall out of a pocket or purse.

6. Gifts are often _____ to people on their birthday.

7. Ferrari cars are _____ by hand, so it takes longer to make them.

8. The watches are _____ into special boxes to protect them.

Grammar: Passive voice with *by*

The passive voice is usually used without a *by* phrase.	Cut flowers **are sold** early in the morning. Most of these cut flowers **are imported.**
A *by* phrase is used when we want to say who or what does something (*the agent*).	These blouses **are made** by well-paid workers. Each rug **is made** by a different artist, so no two rugs are alike.

A Read the sentences and cross out the unimportant *by* phrases.

1. The Mercedes-Benz is made in Germany ~~by people~~.

2. This necklace was given to me by my grandmother.

3. King Tut's tomb was discovered by Howard Carter.

4. My car was stolen on April 19 by someone.

5. The company was founded by the owner's grandfather.

6. Even during the winter, daisies can be grown in greenhouses by workers.

B Re-write each sentence as a question in the passive voice.

1. Children need to be taught good manners.

   Why *do children need to be taught good manners?*

2. Money should be kept in a bank.

   Why _____ ?

3. Good jobs are often given to people with a good education.

   Why _____ ?

4. Hard work is valued as much as education by some employers.

   Why _____ ?

C 🔄 Ask a partner the questions from exercise **B.** Give your own opinions.

Conversation

A 🔊 **5** Close your book and listen to the conversation. According to Gary, why is education valuable?

Lance: Gary, do you think people's lives are improved by money?

Gary: It depends. Some people don't have enough money to buy necessities. Their lives are definitely improved by having more money.

Lance: What about other people?

Gary: Well, when you have enough money for the basics, I think your life can be improved by education.

Lance: Interesting! Is your education improving your life?

Gary: Sure. I enjoy learning about new things, and I hope to get a good job someday because of my education.

Lance: I see what you mean. For me, though, my life would be improved by having a nice car.

Gary: OK, but nice cars cost money. Maybe you should think about getting a job first.

▲ College campus in the spring

B 🔄 Practice the conversation with a partner. Switch roles and practice it again.

C 🔄 **GOAL CHECK** ✔ **Discuss what makes people's lives better**

Do these things improve people's lives? Have a new conversation about each one and add your own idea.

| a big house | fame | nice clothes |
| electronics | good health | _____ |

Real Language

We use *It depends* to say that something is not always true. Then we often explain our reasons.

Reading

A 🔁 Discuss these questions with a partner.

1. Have you ever bought perfume? What brand did you buy?

2. Why do people wear perfume?

3. What do ads for perfume usually show?

B Write answers to the questions.

1. What are the two main ingredients in perfume? _____

2. Why do perfume makers use fixatives?

   _____

3. Which French city is famous for its flower farms? _____

4. What are the four advantages of synthetics? _____

   _____

5. What percentage of new perfumes succeed? _____

C 👥 Make a list of other products designed to make people feel better about themselves. Share your list with the class and talk about whether the products really do what they're supposed to do.

▲ "For me, perfume is an indulgence," says Angie Battaglia, an Austin, Texas, businesswoman who owns 30 scents.

Grasse, France

PERFUME:
THE ESSENCE OF
ILLUSION

"Perfume," says Sophia Grojsman of International Flavors & Fragrances, "is a promise in a bottle." We want to believe. We want to be prettier, richer, and happier than we are. Consider the names of the **fragrances** we buy: Joy, Dolce Vita, Pleasures, White Diamonds, Beautiful. "We sell hope," said Charles Revson, founder of the Revlon cosmetics company.

In terms of chemistry, fragrances are a mixture of **aromatic oils** and alcohol. The "fixatives," or oils, that make a fragrance last a long time, traditionally came from animals. Those have mostly been replaced by **synthetic** chemicals. The other ingredients come from plants, especially flowers.

The area around Grasse, France, is famous for growing flowers. Farmers like Joseph Mul have been producing flowers—including roses, jasmine, and lavender—for centuries. Mul's "rose absolute," the fragrant **liquid** he gets from his roses, sells for $3,650 a pound. "Picking roses will never be done by machine," explains Mul. The roses are carefully collected by hand during the early morning. By ten o' clock, the heat of the sun begins to affect the flowers, and the workers are done for the day. "Labor is 60 percent of the cost," says Mul.

The high cost of natural ingredients is just one of the reasons that perfumers today also use artificial ingredients in their fragrances. In addition, synthetics allow perfumers to use scents that cannot be gotten naturally; for example, the scent from the lilac flower. They allow the use of scents from **rare** or endangered flowers, and they save wild animals from being used for their musk—a kind of fixative. According to perfumer Harry Fremont, "Good fragrance is a balance between naturals and synthetics."

Once perfumers have created a lovely fragrance, it's time for the marketing department to work its magic. The industry spends hundreds of millions of dollars each year to convince people to buy something they don't really need. The success rate for new perfumes is low—only about one in ten is successful, so spending money on advertising is a big risk. It's also the only way to let the world know about a fragrance so enchanting that it can make us believe our dreams will come true.

fragrance *perfume*   **aromatic oils** *pleasant smelling oil*
synthetic *artificial, man-made*   **liquid** *a fluid*   **rare** *unusual, unique*

Flower plantation in Grasse, France

Writing

A Read the information. What are the basic parts of a print advertisement?

> Even in the digital age, many newspapers and magazine are printed on paper. That means "print ads" are still important to companies with a product to sell. Print ads may be expensive, but they allow companies to choose their audience. In addition, the audience can spend as long as they want looking at the ad.
>
> Print ads normally have three things in common: a photograph or other image, a message, and a design—including colors and fonts. A successful print ad does not need to appeal to everyone—only to people who might buy the product.

B You are in charge of marketing a new perfume. Discuss the questions.

1. Who is your target audience? (men or women, young or old, etc.)
2. What kind of photograph might appeal to that audience?
3. What is your message? (What do you want the audience to think or do?)
4. What are some key words to include in your message?

C Write a print ad for your perfume.

D **GOAL CHECK** ✔ **Evaluate the effect of advertising**

Choose a luxury item and talk with a partner about the way it is marketed. What forms of advertising are used? How do the advertisers "convince people to buy something they don't really need"?

Opals mined in Australia

Southern
Australia,
Australia

Before You Watch

A Match each word in blue with its definition in the box.

1. The ground under Coober Pedy contains opals. _____

2. Digging is one thing you can do in the ground. _____

3. The Australian outback is very dry and hot. _____

4. Very beautiful opals can be worth a fortune. _____

5. Miners hope for a big payoff for their hard work. _____

a. area that is far away from cities

b. a large sum of money

c. earth, soil

d. the benefit you get from an action

e. to make a hole by taking away earth

While You Watch

A ▶ Watch the video. Circle each word in the box when you hear it.

digging   fortune
outback   payoff   ground

B ▶ Watch the video again. Circle **T** for *true* or **F** for *false*.

1. About three thousand people live in Coober Pedy.   **T**   **F**

2. Over eighty percent of all opals come from Australia.   **T**   **F**

3. Ninety-five percent of all opals are colorless.   **T**   **F**

4. The hope of a huge payoff motivates people to dig for opals.   **T**   **F**

5. Most people in Coober Pedy make a fortune eventually.   **T**   **F**

Word Focus

miners = people who dig for stones or other minerals

After You Watch / Communication

A Some of the tunnels in Coober Pedy are converted into homes. What might be the advantages and disadvantages of these underground homes? Tell a partner.

B Create a newspaper or Internet job listing for opal miners. Describe the work and the potential rewards. Try to attract new people to Coober Pedy!

Tadpoles swimming in the lily stalks

Look at the photo, answer the questions:

1 What animals are these? Where do they usually live?

2 How do they get their food?

UNIT 8 GOALS

1. Use conditionals to talk about real situations

2. Talk about possible future situations

3. Describe what animals do

4. Discuss a problem in nature

POLAR BEAR (*Ursus maritimus*) The polar bear is one of eight different ___ species of bears. Its ___ habitat is the ice and water near the Arctic Circle. These bears are ___ predators that eat other animals. Their usual ___ prey is other arctic animals, such as seals. They ___ hunt for their food during the day. This bear is ___ wild and is found in the north of Canada. Polar bears are vulnerable, and there are not many of them left. Their habitat is shrinking. If we don't ___ protect these bears, they will become ___ extinct.

Vocabulary

A Read the text.

B Match the words in blue to their meanings.

1. to look for animals and kill them
2. an animal that other animals kill to eat
3. animals that kill other animals
4. the place where an animal usually lives

5. a kind of animal or plant
6. doesn't exist any more, all dead
7. to keep safe from danger
8. in nature, not controlled by people

Grammar: Real conditionals in the future

A Study the sentence and answer the questions.

Condition   Result
If we don't protect these bears, they will become extinct.

1. Is the condition possible or not possible? _____
2. Is the result now or in the future? _____

Real conditionals in the future	
We use the real conditional for situations that can happen in the future.	**If you look** out the train window, **you will see** a group of wild deer.
Conditional sentences have two clauses: the condition clause and the result clause.	Condition: *if* + subject + simple present tense verb Result: subject + *will/be going to* + verb
The condition clause can be at the beginning or end of the sentence.	**If you talk** loudly, the birds will fly away. The birds are going to fly away **if you talk** loudly.

B Complete the sentence with the correct form of the verb in parentheses.

1. If an elephant _____ (live) in a zoo, it _____ (get) bored.

2. We _____ (be) very happy if our team _____ (win).

3. If I _____ (see) a bear in the forest, I _____ (yell) loudly.

4. I _____ (go) to the concert if I _____ (have) enough money for a ticket.

5. If you _____ (sleep, not) enough, you _____ (feel) tired.

C Discuss these situations with a partner. Write sentences to describe them in your notebook. What will happen if . . .

1. polar bears can't find enough food?

2. the polar bear's habitat disappears?

3. people put more polar bears in zoos?

4. people protect polar bears?

5. polar bears become extinct?

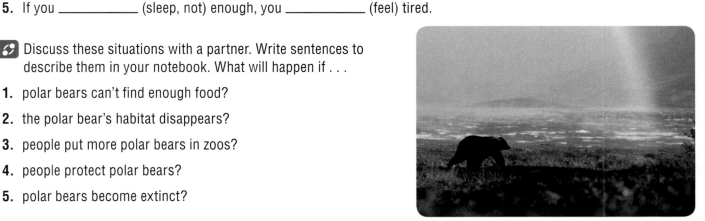

▲ An Alaskan brown bear near Nonvianuk Lake, Katmai National Park, Alaska

Conversation

A 🔊 6 Close your book and listen to the conversation. What is Katie afraid of?

Mike: Let's go camping in the national park.
Katie: I'm not sure that's a good idea. There are black bears in the park.
Mike: That may be, but there aren't very many, and they stay away from people.
Katie: If I see a bear, I'll be really scared. They're so dangerous!
Mike: Bears won't hurt you if you leave them alone.

> **Real Language**
>
> You can say *That may be (true), but . . .* to show that you disagree with the other person's idea.

B Practice the conversation with a partner. Switch roles and practice it again.

C Make two new conversations. Choose from the topics below.

1. White Beach/sharks
2. North Campground/wolves
3. the nature reserve/snakes
4. your own idea _____

D **GOAL CHECK** ✔ **Use conditionals to talk about real situations**

Look at the problems in the box. How will these issues affect nature? Talk about them with a partner.

> climate change
> human population growth
> energy use
> nature shows/other education

These bluefin tuna from a fish farm in the Mediterranean will become sushi in Japanese restaurants.

1. Atlantic Ocean
2. Pacific Ocean
3. Indian Ocean
4. Mediterranean Sea

Listening

A Look at the map and match the places with the boxes on the map.

B 🔊 **7** Listen to the radio program about the bluefin tuna and circle the three places it talks about on the map.

C 🔊 **8** Listen and fill in the blanks.

Bluefin Tuna

1. up to _____ feet long

2. weighs more than _____

3. colors: _____ ,

   _____ , _____

4. swims more than

   _____ miles an hour

5. lives up to

   _____ years

D 🔊 **9** Listen and complete the sentences.

1. In _____ , people use it to make sushi, and in _____ , people love to cook big pieces for tuna steaks.

2. If the boats _____ big bluefins, there _____ young fish in the future.

3. Only _____ of the original population of bluefins was left.

4. If the big boats _____ the fishing in the Mediterranean, many poor people _____ their jobs.

5. If this amazing fish _____ , the seas _____ a great treasure.

E 🗘 Discuss these questions with a partner.

1. Is fish cheap or expensive where you live? How often do you eat it?

2. Do you know where the fish you eat comes from?

Pronunciation: Phrases in sentences

A 🔊 **10** Listen and repeat the sentences. Notice how they're divided into phrases.

1. A bluefin tuna | can swim very fast | and live a long time.

2. My friend's birthday | is June fourteenth.

B Draw lines to divide these sentences into phrases.

1. Jeff and I saw three big sharks.

2. Cathy isn't here, but I can take a message.

3. I'll bring my camera if we go to the zoo.

4. If they catch all the big fish, the species won't survive.

5. The family will have fun at the national park.

C 🔊 **11** Listen and check your answers. Practice saying the sentences.

Communication

A Read the information. What does *sustainable* mean?

Fish is one of the world's favorite foods. Around the world, the average person eats 36 pounds (16 kg) of fish every year. But many kinds of fish around the world are disappearing because people catch too many of them. Scientists say that 90 percent of the biggest fish are gone now. If we catch too many big fish now, there won't be any baby fish in the future. Our way of fishing now is not **sustainable**—it can't continue for a long time without hurting the environment.

> ### Word Focus
>
> The word **environment** can refer to nature or to everything that's around us.
>
> *Recycling used paper is good for the **environment.***
>
> *This classroom is a good **environment** for learning.*

B 👥 You are members of an environmental group called **Save the Oceans.** You want to take action to solve the fishing problem. Talk about these plans. What will happen if we follow each one?

Plan A: Don't eat fish!	Plan B: Safe fish symbol	Plan C: Strict laws about fishing
Tell people to stop buying and eating fish. Put ads in newspapers and magazines, and make TV commercials to explain why fishing hurts the environment.	Make a special symbol for fish that are caught in a sustainable way. Make commercials to tell people to look for this symbol in supermarkets and restaurants.	Make stronger laws about how many fish people can catch. Send special police in fast boats to all of the fishing areas to make sure that fishing boats follow the laws.

C 👥 **GOAL CHECK** ✓ **Talk about possible future situations**

Which is the best plan? Why? Explain your decision to the class.

Language Expansion: Adverbs of manner

A 🔁 How do they do it? Complete the sentences with an adverb from the box.

| beautifully | fast | well |
| slowly | loudly | badly |

1. A snail moves ___slowly___ .

2. A fox hunts _____ .

3. A penguin walks _____ .

4. A monkey jumps _____ .

5. A lion roars _____ .

6. A bird sings _____ .

Adverbs of manner	
Adverbs of manner tell us how an action is done. The adverb usually follows the verb.	A snail <u>moves</u> **slowly.** Tigers <u>run</u> **fast.**
Many adverbs of manner are formed from adjectives plus -*ly*.	quick – quickly safe – safely soft – softly careful – carefully
Some adverbs of manner are irregular.	well fast hard
Note: For most adjectives that end in -*y*, change the -*y* to -*i* and add -*ly*.	easy – easily happy – happily angry – angrily

| quick | careful |
| quiet | easy | loud |

B 🔁 In your notebook, write sentences using the adverb form of each adjective in the box.

Grammar: Review of quantifiers

A 🔁 Write C for count nouns or NC for non-count nouns.

Raccoons are small (1) _____ <u>animals</u> that live in North America, Japan, and a few (2) _____ <u>parts</u> of Europe. They are *omnivores*—animals that eat both plants and animals. A raccoon's usual diet is (3) _____ <u>nuts</u> and (4) _____ <u>fruit</u>. They also like to eat insects. Sometimes they catch (5) _____ <u>fish</u> or (6) _____ <u>frogs</u>.

Quantifiers					
With count nouns			**With non-count nouns**		
too few a few some	a lot of many too many	eggs	too little a little some	a lot of too much	meat

*Quantifiers tell us *how much* or *how many*.
*Don't use *much* in affirmative sentences: ~~He has much money~~. He has a lot of money.

B Circle the correct quantifier in each sentence below.

1. Raccoons eat (many | a little) different kinds of food.

2. They eat (a little | a lot of) nuts.

3. Raccoons will eat (a few | a little) insects if they find them.

4. They sometimes eat (a little | many) soap.

5. If a raccoon goes in your garbage can, you'll find (a lot of | many) garbage all over the place!

Conversation

A 🔊 **12** Listen to the conversation with your book closed. What does the woman want to see at the zoo?

Dan: So, which animals do you want to see at the zoo?
Carmen: I love to look at the penguins. I think they're really amazing.
Dan: Why is that?
Carmen: Well, they walk so slowly, but in the water they swim really well. And it's fun to watch them at feeding time.
Dan: Really? What do they eat?
Carmen: They eat a lot of fish and a few shrimp.

B 🔁 Practice the conversation with a partner. Switch roles and practice it again.

C 🔁 Fill in the chart. Add your own ideas. Then make new conversations.

	What they do	What they eat
1. tigers		
2. elephants		

meat   walk   play
leaves   grass   swim
run   fruit

D ♻ **GOAL CHECK** ✓ **Describe what animals do**

Report to the class. Tell them about your favorite zoo animal. Try to use adverbs and quantifiers.

Reading

A 🔁 What are some reasons animals are endangered? Talk about your ideas with a partner.

B 🔁 Look at the list of ways we can protect endangered animals. Check (✓) the ideas you predict you will read about in the article. Compare your answers with a partner.

1. _____ stop poaching

2. _____ create advertisements about conservation

3. _____ prevent droughts

4. _____ put land under conservation

5. _____ support nature tourism

C Read the article. Write the dates next to the events.

1. _____ 20 lions remain in Kunene

2. _____ John Kasaona is born

3. _____ drought hits Namibia

4. _____ war begins

5. _____ war ends

D 🔁 List two good things in your notebook about the community-based conservation program. Compare your answers with a partner.

Many elephants are killed for their tusks.

John Kasaona
Community-Based Conservationist

HOW POACHERS BECAME CARETAKERS

When John Kasaona was a boy growing up in Namibia, his father took him into the **bush** to teach him how to take care of the family's livestock. His father said, "If you see a cheetah eating our goat, walk up to it and smack it on the backside." A cheetah is a very nervous animal. If a person **confronts** it, it will probably run away. John also learned how to deal with a lion by standing very still and making himself look very big. These were useful lessons for a boy who became a wildlife **conservationist.** As Kasaona says, "It is very important if you are in the field to know what to confront and what to run from."

Kasaona was born in 1971. At that time, Namibia had many problems. The country was at war from 1966 to 1990. Because of the fighting, many people had rifles. This caused a secondary problem—**poaching.** For example, poachers killed many black rhinos for their horns, which were very valuable. To make things even worse, around 1980, a terrible drought killed people, livestock, and wildlife. By 1995, there were only 20 lions left in the Kunene region in the northwest of the country, where Kasaona's family lives. Many other **species** were also endangered.

At the same time, positive changes were taking place. A non-governmental organization, the Integrated Rural Development and Nature Conservation (IRDNC), began working in Namibia to protect wildlife. They met with village leaders to ask who would be able to work with them. They needed people who knew the bush well and who understood how wild animals lived. The

> **We knew conservation would fail if it didn't work to improve the lives of the local communities.**
>
> — John Kasaona

John Kasaona's idea worth spreading is that there is good news from Africa. Protecting wildlife is a great way to transform communities — and countries. Watch Kasaona's full TED Talk on TED.com.

answer was surprising: work with local poachers. It seemed crazy, but it also made sense. After all, if you spend your time hunting for animals, you will know where they live and how they behave. So IRDNC hired a group of poachers, including Kasaona's own father, to help protect wildlife in Namibia.

Since then, the situation has changed dramatically. The Kunene region now has more than 130 lions. The black rhino, almost extinct in 1982, has come back, and there are now many free-roaming black rhinos in Kunene. Most importantly, more land than ever is under conservation. That protected land generates money from tourism for Namibia to use in education, health care, and other important programs for its people.

John Kasaona explains, "We were successful in Namibia because we dreamed of a future that was much more than just a healthy wildlife." Kasaona created a model for other nations to follow by starting the largest community-led conservation program in the world.

---

bush *land far from towns and cities*
confront *to challenge (someone) in a forceful way*
conservationist *someone who works to protect animals, plants, and natural resources*
poaching *killing an animal illegally*
species *a group of animals or plants that are similar*

Poaching endangers species in their natural habitats.

Communication

A Think about two or three problems in nature in your country. What is happening? What are the causes? Share your ideas with a partner.

Writing

A Complete the sentences about a problem in nature in your country.

1. If we believe in conservation, we will _____.

2. If _____, many animals will be saved.

3. If people want to make positive changes, they will _____.

B Write *but, so,* and *even though* in the correct places in the paragraph.

By the 1990s, many species of animals were endangered in Namibia.

The situation was serious, (1)_____ conservationists needed

to find a way to protect the animals. They found one, (2)_____

it wasn't what you would expect: they asked poachers for help.

(3)_____ this seemed crazy, I think it was a great idea. If we want

to protect endangered species, we need to consider every solution.

C Write a paragraph in your notebook giving your opinion about a problem in nature in your country. Be sure to use the connectors in Exercise **B.**

Writing Strategy

Conjunctions

Conjunctions are used to connect ideas within sentences.

D **GOAL CHECK** ✔ Discuss a problem in nature

Work with a group. Share your ideas from Exercise **A** about problems in nature. In your opinion, what is the most important problem to solve? What are two or three ways to help?

Elephants crossing Luangwa River, Loxodonta africana, Zambia

Before You Watch

A 🔁 Read about the video and check the meanings of the words in **bold** with a partner.

While You Watch

A ▶ Watch the video *Happy Elephants*. Choose the main idea.

1. Elephants are happier in the wild.

2. People and elephants have been together for a long time.

3. Elephant trainers find ways to make elephants happier.

B ▶ Watch the video again. Fill in the information.

1. Elephants and people have worked together for over _____ years.

2. There is one question that people have been asking: How is it possible to keep

    elephants happy? _____

3. Many people who work closely with animals say that they do have

    _____ and can experience happiness.

4. That means that they live in families and herds and they _____
    other elephants.

5. For elephants, communication and social relationships are really

    _____ .

After You Watch

A 🔁 Discuss these questions with your partner. Have you visited a zoo or seen a video of a zoo? Do you think the animals like living there? Why or why not?

> Elephants are amazing animals. They can use their **trunks** to pick up heavy things. **In the wild,** they live in **herds** in the forest. Today, many elephants live in zoos. Their **trainers** take care of them. But can elephants be happy **in captivity**?

The ancient city of Petra, Jordan at night

UNIT 9 GOALS

1. Discuss life in the past

2. Contrast different ways of life

3. Compare today with the past

4. Talk about a historical wonder

▲ Marco Polo

▲ Ibn Battuta

▲ Zheng He

Vocabulary

A Read the information about three early travelers.

Long-distance travel can be difficult for anyone, but it used to be even more challenging. Yet despite the difficulty, people have always wanted to see and learn about distant regions. These three brave explorers did exactly that— hundreds of years ago! The result was an exchange of knowledge and culture that changed the world.

Marco Polo (1254–1324) We don't know exactly when and where Marco Polo was born, but he lived in Venice and Genoa, in what is now Italy, and he traveled east—far beyond the borders of Europe into Asia. The stories he published after his travels seem to mix together fact and fiction, but they inspired other European explorers, including Christopher Columbus.

Ibn Battuta (1304–1369) Ibn Battuta was a remarkable traveler. Born in Morocco, he visited most of the Muslim world—North Africa, the Middle East, and East Africa—as well as South Asia, including Sri Lanka and India, and even China. Battuta's goal was to search for knowledge and new experiences, and his stories taught people about other parts of the world at a time when few people traveled.

Zheng He (1371–1433) The explorations of Zheng He took him by sea from China west to the Middle East and Africa. According to stories, Zheng commanded enormous ships more than 400 feet (122 m) long—much, much larger than other ships of the time. The size of the ships was probably helpful for trade, as well as for carrying military people and equipment.

B Write each word in blue next to the correct definition or synonym.

1. _____ look for
2. _____ impressive
3. _____ buying and selling
4. _____ past a limit
5. _____ giving and taking
6. _____ large boats

7. _____ far away
8. _____ printed copies of writing
9. _____ gave enthusiasm or ideas
10. _____ even though

Word Focus

Use **even though** before a clause with a subject and verb.

Use **despite** before a noun or noun phrase.

*They traveled **even though** it was difficult.*

*They traveled **despite** the difficulty.*

Grammar: *Used to*

We use *used to* + base form of a verb to talk about the past.	My father **used to** build ships, but now he is retired from his job.
Used to usually shows a contrast between past and present.	The company **used to** publish travel books. (Now they publish cookbooks.)
In questions and negative statements, use *did/didn't* + *use to*.	**Did** people **use to** see pictures of distant places? They **didn't use to** know much about other places and cultures.

A Complete each sentence with *used to* plus the verb in parentheses and your own ideas.

1. My grandparents _____ (travel) a lot. Now they _____ .
2. Train tickets _____ (be) cheap. Now they _____ .
3. I _____ (find) information at the library. Now I _____ .
4. She _____ (take) pictures with a camera. Now she _____ .
5. People _____ (write) letters. Now they _____ .

B Complete the conversations with the words in the box.

Sue: Why did people (1) _____ to travel by horse?

Aki: Well, there (2) _____ use to be other transportation.

Sue: OK, but did everyone use to (3) _____ that way?

Aki: Why do you ask? You didn't use to (4) _____ about horses.

Sue: I'm writing about transportation in the past, so I need to include horses.

Aki: You should talk to Mr. Clark. He (5) _____ to ride horses when he was younger, and he knows a lot about them.

> care didn't use
> travel used

Conversation

A 🔊 **13** Close your book and listen to the conversation. How old are the El Tajín ruins?

Ben: What's up, Patricia?
Patricia: Not much. I'm looking at pictures of the El Tajín ruins in Mexico.
Ben: I've never heard of El Tajín.
Patricia: It's a remarkable archaeological site that's over a thousand years old. It has several buildings, some pyramids, ball courts . . .
Ben: Ball courts? Why are there ball courts?
Patricia: Well, people used to play ball games there. El Tajín was a center of culture and government, and the games were part of the culture.
Ben: Ball games? That's interesting!
Patricia: It is, and there are at least 20 ball courts on the site!
Ben: Are they used for anything today?
Patricia: Actually, people go to El Tajín now for concerts and events.

▲ El Tajín in Veracruz, Mexico

B 🗣 Practice the conversation with a partner. Then describe the historical places in the box or other places you know about. What used to happen at these places? What happens there now?

> The pyramids at Giza
> Stonehenge in England
> The Colosseum in Rome

C 🗣 **GOAL CHECK** ✔ **Discuss life in the past**

How has modern technology changed people's lives? Tell your partner what people used to do in the past, and what they do now. Use the topics in the box and your own ideas.

> transportation
> communication
> home life entertainment

Sami reindeer herder
in Northern Europe

Listening

A Look at the map on this page. How do you think people used to live in this part of the world 1,000 years ago? Check (✓) the things you think people did.

1. _____ ate fish from the Arctic Ocean

2. _____ lived on small farms

3. _____ followed groups of animals, such as reindeer

4. _____ lived in houses made of wood

5. _____ had their own language and customs

B 🔊 **14** Listen to a talk about the Sami people and choose the main idea.

a. The Sami people depend on animals, especially reindeer, to make a living.

b. Life is changing for the Sami people, but some of them live in traditional ways.

c. Many young Sami people want to attend a university and choose a career.

C 🔊 **14** Listen again and circle **T** for *true* or **F** for *false*. Correct the false sentences to make them true.

1. Traditionally, the Sami people stayed and lived in one place.　　**T**　**F**

2. Reindeer were used by the Sami people for food and clothing.　　**T**　**F**

3. Most Sami people still live in the traditional way.　　**T**　**F**

4. Some Sami people now raise reindeer on farms.　　**T**　**F**

5. New laws affect the way Sami people may use land.　　**T**　**F**

Word Focus

Some animal words don't have plural forms:

deer　reindeer　sheep　bison

D 🔁 Do you think it's important to maintain traditions from the past? Or do you think people should focus on the future? Discuss your ideas with a partner.

Pronunciation: Reduction of *used to*

When we speak quickly, *used to* is sometimes pronounced /yU-st(ə)/.

A 🔊 **15** You will hear each sentence twice. Listen to the full form and the reduced form of *used to*. Listen again and repeat the sentences.

1. People used to make their own clothes.
2. They used to hunt animals and catch fish.
3. Did you use to play baseball?
4. Food used to cost a lot less.
5. My grandfather used to read to me.

B 🔁 Complete the sentences with your own information. Then read the sentences aloud to a partner. Use the reduced form /yU-st(ə)/.

1. When I was younger, I used to _____ .
2. As a child, I used to want money for _____ .
3. In my country, people used to _____ .
4. Before I was born, my grandparents used to _____ .
5. As children, my parents used to _____ .

Communication

A 🔁 How is life today different than it was 50 years ago? Tell your partner at least four things people used to do and what they do now.

> **People used to make phone calls at home. Now they use cell phones anywhere.**

> **True, and their conversations used to be private. Now everyone can hear them!**

B 🔁 How has your life changed over the years? Tell your partner at least four things you didn't use to know or do.

> **I didn't use to speak English. Now I speak it every day.**

> **I didn't use to get along with my brother. Now we're friends.**

▲ Old Russian telephone in Norway

C 🔁 **GOAL CHECK** ✔ **Contrast different ways of life**

Discuss the differences between the traditional Sami lifestyle and the way most Sami people live today. Consider housing, food, education, language, and transportation.

Language Expansion: Separable phrasal verbs

A Some phrasal verbs are used more frequently than one-word verbs. Complete the paragraph with the phrasal verb closest in meaning to the verb in parentheses.

> bring up   help out   turn on   bring back   put on   figure out

Hi, my name is Susie, and I live in the Nunavut Territory in Canada. Life in Nunavut hasn't changed as much as it has in other places. It's true—nowadays, we can (1)_____ (start) the furnace when it gets cold instead of building a fire, but we haven't given up our traditional culture. We still (2)_____ (raise) our children in the land our people have lived in for thousands of years. We teach them to (3)_____ (don) our traditional clothing to stay warm in the winter. When they're old enough, we teach them to (4)_____ (discover, solve) solutions to everyday problems. We teach them to (5)_____ (return) anything they borrow. And most importantly, we teach them to always (6)_____ (aid) their family and their community. Those things will never change.

B 🗘 Answer the questions. Use pronouns and the separable phrasal verbs.

1. What can you do with children?
2. What can you do with shoes?
3. How can you assist your friends?
4. How can you understand something?
5. What can you do with a borrowed book?
6. What can you do when a computer is turned off?

Grammar: Passive voice in the past

Passive voice in the past	
Use the active voice in the past to focus on the subject of a sentence.	Parents **raised** their children differently in the past.
Use the passive voice in the past to focus on the object or receiver of a past action.	Children **were raised** differently in the past (by their parents).
Form the past passive with *was* or *were* + the past participle of a verb.	My father **was taught** to always tell the truth.

Word Focus

Separable phrasal verbs can be separated by an object—usually a pronoun.

We **set up** a tent to sleep in.
We **set it up** over there.

> **What can you do with children?**

> **You can bring them up.**

Regular past participles:
invent – invented
pull – pulled
hunt – hunted

Irregular past participles:
eat – eaten
drink – drunk
sell – sold

A Complete each sentence with the past passive form of the verb in parentheses.

1. Large stones _____ (use) to build the Egyptian pyramids.
2. Igloos _____ (build) from blocks of ice by the Inuit people.
3. Writing _____ (invent) in Mesopotamia.
4. Wild animals _____ (hunt) by Native Americans.
5. Chocolate _____ (drink) by the Aztecs.

B How did things get done in the past in your country? Complete each sentence with the past passive form of the verb in parentheses and your own ideas.

1. People _____ (tell) about important news by _____.
2. Children _____ (teach) by _____.
3. Clothes _____ (make) by _____.
4. Important books _____ (publish) by _____.
5. People _____ (inspire) by _____.

▲ An Inuit man builds an igloo.

Conversation

A ◄))) **16** Close your books and listen to the conversation. What does Luisa want to find out?

Luisa: Hi, Carl. Can I ask you a question?
Carl: Sure. Go ahead.
Luisa: Do you think we really need to study history?
Carl: Of course we do! A lot of important things happened in the past.
Luisa: Like what?
Carl: Well, different systems of government were developed.
Luisa: OK, those are important. What else?
Carl: A lot of remarkable technology was invented—like the telephone.
Luisa: Yes, that's very important!
Carl: And scientific discoveries were made in the past, too.
Luisa: You're right. I do want to know more about the past.
Carl: Good—have fun in your history class!

B Practice the conversation with a partner. Switch roles and practice again. Then make new conversations using your own ideas to answer Luisa's questions.

C **GOAL CHECK** ✔ **Compare today with the past**

Talk to a partner. How were things done before the following services were developed, and how are they done now?

public transportation **city water systems** **garbage collection service**

Reading

A 🔁 What do you know about Genghis Khan? Check (✓) the information you think is true. Compare your answers with your partner.

_____ He had a difficult childhood.

_____ He was a wise leader and a talented general.

_____ He lived in Central Asia in the eighteenth century.

_____ He conquered many kingdoms and destroyed their cities.

_____ His empire lasted for hundreds of years.

B Read the sentences and circle **T** for _true_ or **F** for _false_.

1. After the Mongol attack, Samarkand was a ruined city.   **T**   **F**

2. The Mongol Empire covered only a small area.   **T**   **F**

3. Modern Mongolians think of Genghis Khan as an important leader.   **T**   **F**

4. Genghis Khan became the leader of his people when he was around 40 years old.   **T**   **F**

5. People haven't been able to find Genghis Khan's tomb because his soldiers burned it after he was buried.   **T**   **F**

C 🔁 Discuss these questions with a partner. How was Central Asia different after the Mongol Empire? In your opinion, were the changes positive or negative? Give reasons for your answer.

LORD OF THE MONGOLS

When the Mongol leader Genghis Khan arrived in 1220, Samarkand was one of Central Asia's greatest cities, with about 200,000 people. Today, there is nothing left of the old city. A visitor can see only grass, ridges, and hills shaped by the wind.

Again and again in the thirteenth century, Mongol armies rode into Central Asia and destroyed its cities, killed its people, and took its treasure. The world has rarely seen so much destruction, but it built one of the world's greatest empires. By 1280, the Mongols controlled territory from the Yellow Sea to the Mediterranean.

The question people usually ask about the Mongols is: Were they only **raiders** and killers? Not in Mongolian eyes. In Mongolia, Genghis is like George Washington; he was the first ruler of united Mongolia. In China, his grandson Kublai is admired for unifying the country. It is also true that the Mongols killed without mercy. They killed opposing armies as well as civilians.

Genghis Khan was born in the 1160s. He was originally named Temujin. When Temujin was born, Mongolia had about thirty **nomadic tribes.** His father was the leader of a small tribe, but he was killed by another tribe when Temujin was only nine. Afterwards, the family struggled to survive.

Despite his difficult beginnings, Temujin grew to be a great **warrior.** He destroyed the enemy tribe that killed his father. In 1206, after many battles, Temujin became Genghis Khan, a name meaning "strong ruler" or "oceanic ruler." In other words, he was ruler of the world. He was about 40 years old.

In August 1227, Genghis died. He was probably 60. Stories say his body was buried in Mongolia, near a mountain called Burkhan Khaldun. Forty beautiful young women and forty horses were buried with him. A thousand horsemen are said to have ridden over the site until it could not be found. It still eludes people who are searching for it.

raider *a person who suddenly attacks a place or group* **nomadic** *people who move from place to place* **tribe** *people with the same language, customs, and beliefs* **warrior** *a person who fights and is known for having courage and skill*

Many Mongolians are still nomadic and still live in an easily moveable *ger.*

Taj Mahal in Agra, Uttar Pradesh, India

Bernard Weber wanted to use modern technology to bring the people of the world closer together. He knew that the original Seven Wonders of the Ancient World were chosen by one person, and six of the wonders didn't even exist anymore, so he created a way to let the world determine the New 7 Wonders: an open election using the Internet and text messaging. Anyone could nominate a special site, and anyone could vote.

Millions of votes were cast, and on July 7, 2007, the seven winners were announced in Lisbon, Portugal. They include the Great Wall of China, the Colosseum in Rome, and the Taj Mahal in India. More recently, Weber's Internet-based project has used voting to choose the New 7 Wonders of nature and New 7 Wonders Cities.

Communication

A Discuss the questions with a partner.

1. Which words describe your reaction to historical wonders? Explain your choices and add another word of your own.

> amazed   interested   proud   shocked   inspired   _____

2. Tell your partner about some of the historical wonders from your country. What amazing things did people do in the past?

Writing

A Read the information in the box about the New 7 Wonders of the World.

B Use the Internet to research one of the New 7 Wonders historical sites. Write a paragraph with interesting information about the site. Use your own words, including adjectives, to describe your reaction to the site.

C **GOAL CHECK** ✓ **Talk about a historical wonder**

Share your paragraph with a partner. Talk about the information that is interesting or surprising to you.

Albert Lin in Mongolia

Before You Watch

A Discuss the questions with a partner. Who is Genghis Khan? Where is he from, and why is he famous? Where do people think Genghis Khan is buried? How is Albert Lin going to find his tomb?

B Fill in the blanks with the correct words from the box.

1. Albert Lin is using the most advanced, or _____, technology to find Genghis Khan's tomb.

2. Genghis Khan was buried in a part of Mongolia that is called the _____ Zone, where very few outsiders visit.

3. Because many Mongolians believe Genghis's tomb is _____, or holy, Lin and his team can't dig there.

4. Instead, they are using _____, which detect heat, light, sound, and motion.

> cutting-edge
> Forbidden   sacred
> sensors

While You Watch

A Read the sentences and circle **T** for *true* or **F** for *false*.

1. Albert Lin and his team are working only from the United States to find Genghis's tomb.   **T**   **F**

2. Lin always planned to be an explorer.   **T**   **F**

3. Lin wants to dig up Genghis's tomb and remove the treasure inside.   **T**   **F**

4. Many non-scientists are helping with the research by examining satellite images.   **T**   **F**

After You Watch / Communication

A Make predictions with a partner about how new technology can be used in exploration and research. Think about exploration on land, under the sea, and in space.

TEDTALKS

Before You Watch

A Look at the picture and answer the questions with a partner.

1. What kind of animal is in the photo?

2. Where do these animals live?

3. What else do you know about these animals and their habitat?

B Look at the words in the box. Complete the paragraph with the correct word. Not all words will be used.

> **collectively** *adj.* shared or done by a group of people
> **condone** *v.* to allow (something that is considered wrong) to continue
> **crash** *v.* to go down very suddenly and quickly
> **disrupt** *v.* to cause (something) to be unable to continue in the normal way
> **pride** *n.* a group of lions
> **revenue stream** *n.* a flow of money that is made by or paid to a business or an organization

Africa's big cats are endangered, and we are all (1) _____ responsible. Soon, the (2) _____ of lions may disappear. Because we (3) _____ hunting and other activities that put them at risk, their numbers

Beverly and Dereck Jouberts' idea worth spreading is that not only do big cats like lions and leopards have big personalities, but getting to know them can help protect Africa. Watch the Jouberts' full TED Talk on TED.com.

have (4) _____ in the last 50 years. And it's not only the big cats that are in danger—ecotourism brings in a large (5) _____ to Africa. If the cats disappear, so will the money and jobs.

C Beverly and Dereck Joubert are wildlife photographers who publicize the problem of endangered big cats. What do you predict you will hear in their TED Talk? Look at the pictures on the next page. Check (✓) the information you predict you will hear.

_____ **1.** They have spent five years watching a leopard cub grow up.

_____ **2.** They are also researching the behavior of giraffes and elephants.

_____ **3.** Their investigations have shown that these lions are essential.

_____ **4.** Lion bones are being sold.

While You Watch

A Watch the TED Talk. Circle the main idea.

1. It's necessary to study big cats over many years.

2. If the big cats disappear, many other species may disappear.

3. Beverly and Dereck Joubert believe that big cats are beautiful.

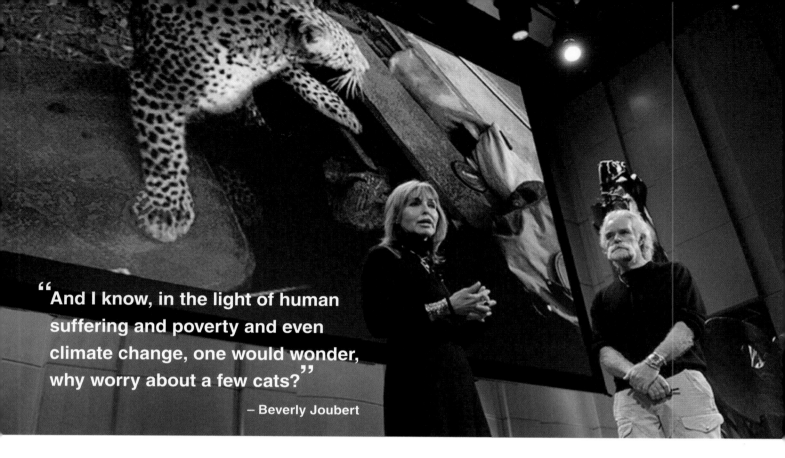

"And I know, in the light of human suffering and poverty and even climate change, one would wonder, why worry about a few cats?"

– Beverly Joubert

B ▶ Watch the TED Talk again and match the photo that illustrates the TED Talk to the correct caption.

_____ **a.** If a male lion is killed, the members of his pride may also die.

_____ **b.** The Jouberts have discovered that some lions hunt in the water.

_____ **c.** Legadema trusts the Jouberts and lets them come close to her.

_____ **d.** The Jouberts have studied a young leopard named Legadema since she was a baby.

1.

2.

3.

4.

TEDTALKS

Beverly and Dereck Joubert Documentary Filmmakers/ Conservationists, National Geographic Explorers-in-Residence
LIFE LESSONS FROM BIG CATS

After You Watch

A Complete the summary with the words in the box.

> extinction   passionate   photographing   respect   survive

Beverly and Dereck Joubert are (1) _____ about protecting the African wilderness. They have spent many years studying and (2) _____ big cats. In the last 50 years, these cats have been pushed to the edge of (3) _____ by hunters. The Jouberts believe that if the big cats are viewed with (4) _____, they can survive. And if the big cats (5) _____, they can help us maintain our connection to nature and to other human beings.

B Match the phrases to the information from the video.

_____ **1.** number of lions alive now

_____ **2.** number of leopards left in the wild

_____ **3.** years the Jouberts have been filming big cats

_____ **4.** amount of ecotourism revenue stream

_____ **5.** number of years the Jouberts followed Legadema

a. $80 billion

b. 5

c. 20,000

d. 50,000

e. 28

C Read the statements below. Circle the ones that paraphrase information in the TED Talk.

1. Many kinds of big cats live in the African wilderness.

2. It's important to protect big cats and the humans who live near them.

3. There used to be more than 450,000 lions in Africa.

4. It is wrong to hunt and kill lions for sport.

5. If we aren't connected to nature, we will lose hope.

Project

Beverly and Dereck Joubert want to protect the African wilderness. Use their ideas to write a letter in support of big cat conservation to the editor of a newspaper in your country. Follow these steps.

D Work with a partner to find facts and opinions from the TED Talk that you can include. Complete the chart below. Choose the ones that support your idea the best.

FACT	OPINION

E Write your letter. Use the frame below to organize your ideas. Then show your letter to a different partner. Is your opinion easy to understand? Does he or she have ideas for improvement?

To the Editor:

I am writing to (1) _____. In my opinion, (2) _____. If we don't

(3) _____, we will (4) _____. It is also important to (5) _____. We

will (6) _____ if we (7) _____.

Finally, I think (8) _____. If (9) _____, then (10) _____.

Yours sincerely,

_____

Challenge! Beverly and Dereck Joubert are working to ensure the long-term survival of big cats. Find out more about the Big Cats Initiative at TED.com and explore ways you can get involved. Share what you learn with the class.

Travel

Dead camelthorn trees with hikers in
Namib-Naukluft National Park, Namibia

Look at the photo, answer the questions:

1 Where do you think these people are? What are they doing?

2 What type of trip would you like to take? Why?

UNIT 10 GOALS

1. Talk about preparations for a trip

2. Talk about different kinds of vacations

3. Use English at the airport

4. Discuss the pros and cons of tourism

Vocabulary

A Label each picture with the correct phrase in the box.

talk to the **travel agent**
apply for a **passport**
apply for a **visa**
buy a **ticket**
make a **reservation**
check the **itinerary**
get **sightseeing** information
get a **vaccination**

_____ _____ _____ _____

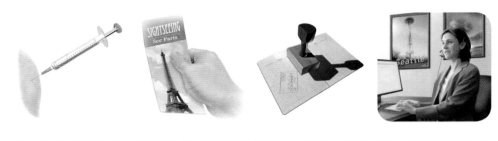

_____ _____ _____ _____

B What did you do before your last trip? Use vocabulary from exercise **A**.

Grammar: Expressing necessity

Use *must* + verb in writing or formal speaking to say that something is necessary or is a rule.	Travelers **must apply** for a passport at least six weeks in advance.
Use *have to* or *need to* + verb in informal speaking. Use *have (got) to* + verb for extra emphasis.	We **have to buy** our tickets. I **need to get** a vaccination. Jerry **has got to make** a hotel reservation soon!
Use *don't have to* + verb to say that something is not necessary.	You **don't have to buy** a ticket for a baby. Babies can ride the train for free.
Have to and *need to* can be used with different verb tenses.	We **had to show** them our passports. Someone **will need to** carry Lin's bag.

A Circle the correct option for each sentence.

1. Everyone (got to | needs to) get a vaccination before the trip.

2. You can't change your reservation online. You (must | will must) talk to a travel agent.

3. Last week, we (need to | had to) apply for a visa.

4. To get a driver's license, you (must | don't have to) pass a driving test.

5. Abdul (has got to | have to) apply for a passport now!

6. You (haven't to | don't have to) make reservations for the train.

Word Focus

a **plane/train/hotel reservation**
a **plane/train/bus ticket**

Ayers Rock, Australia

B Look at the car rental rules in the chart. Work with a partner to make sentences using expressions of necessity.

C What are the rules in your English class? Write a list in your notebook. Use expressions of necessity. Compare your list with a partner's list.

1. You **have to** hand in your homework.

Conversation

A 🔊 17 Close your book and listen to the conversation. Where is Peter going on his vacation?

Ed: So, Peter, when are you taking your vacation?
Peter: In September. I'm going to South Africa.
Ed: Wow, South Africa! What a great trip!
Peter: It will be. But first I have to get a new passport, and I have to apply for a visa.
Ed: That sounds like a hassle!
Peter: It's not so bad. I can get the visa from my travel agent. And I don't have to get any vaccinations.

B Practice the conversation with a partner. Switch roles and practice again.

C Look at the chart. Make new conversations about these countries.

Do travelers need . . .	a passport?	a visa?	vaccinations?
Turkey	Yes	Yes (online)	No
Australia	Yes	Yes (from the embassy)	No
The Philippines	Yes	No	No

D **GOAL CHECK** ✔ **Talk about preparations for a trip**

Talk to a partner. Say where you want to go and what you need to do to prepare for the trip.

Car rental rules	
have a driver's license	☑
make a reservation	☒
tell the company where you're going	☒
be 25 years old	☑
pay with a credit card	☑

> **You have to have a driver's license.**

Real Language

A *hassle* is an informal word for "problem" or "trouble."

Listening

A 🔗 Read the information. Tell your partner which kind of vacation you would enjoy the most. Explain.

1. Adventure vacation	2. Relaxing vacation	3. Learning vacation
Try exciting sports, like mountain climbing, bicycling, and skiing. Have experiences to tell your friends about.	Go to a beautiful place to rest and relax. Sleep late, read, listen to music, and enjoy the scenery.	Learn to do something new, like art or music, or take a class in a subject that interests you.

B 🔊 18 Listen to three people talking about their vacations. Which country are they going to?

Carla: _____

Marcus: _____

Julie: _____

C 🔊 18 Listen again. Which kind of vacation will they take?

Carla: _____

Marcus: _____

Julie: _____

D 🔗 Which of these vacations would you enjoy the most? Explain your reasons to your partner.

Pronunciation: Reduction of *have to, has to, got to*

A 🔊 19 Listen to the pronunciation of *have to, has to,* and *got to.* Notice how they sound like *hafta, hasta,* and *gotta* in fast speech.

> I've **got to** finish my homework. (sounds like /ga-ɾə/)
> He **has to** clean the house. (sounds like /hæ-stə/)
> Do you **have to** work tomorrow? (sounds like /hæ-ftə/)

B 🔗 Practice these sentences with a partner. Pay attention to the pronunciation of *have to, has to,* and *got to.*

1. Sorry, I have to leave now.
2. I've got to apply for a visa.
3. Rosa has to pack her suitcase.
4. They've got to stay after class.
5. He has to be there at six o'clock.
6. Do you have to make a reservation?
7. You've got to answer my questions.
8. Tomorrow, I have to go to the bank.

Adventure tour in Africa! Travel from Egypt to South Africa in a truck and visit twenty countries. You'll see wildlife and learn about African cultures.

Communication

You and a partner have won a dream vacation in a contest. Read about the three different trips.

Live with a family in London, and take English classes at a language school with students from many countries. Every weekend, you'll take a trip to a famous place.

Stay in a beach house! Swim, relax, or just do nothing. The house has a beautiful garden with a view of the sea, and a chef will cook all of your meals.

A 🔁 Talk with a partner about the three trips and choose which one you will take together.

B 🔁 What do you have to do before this trip? Think of five things.

C 🔁 What will you take along? List fifteen things.

D ♻ **GOAL CHECK** ✔ **Talk about different kinds of vacations**

Get together with another pair of students. Tell them about your plans. Why did you choose this trip instead of the other two? Explain your reasons.

> If we go to Africa, we'll have to get lots of vaccinations!

> I'll bring a digital camera to take pictures of the animals.

Language Expansion: At the airport

| 1. departures |
| 2. security check |
| 3. gate |
| 4. terminal |
| 5. boarding pass |
| 6. airline agent |
| 7. baggage claim |
| 8. carry-on bag |

A Write the numbers of the words from the box in the correct circles.

B Complete the sentences. Use the words from exercise **A**.

1. At the _____ , officers look inside your bags.

2. You can take a small _____ on the plane with you.

3. After your flight, get your bags from the _____ .

4. The _____ looks at your ticket and gives you a seat.

5. When you are going somewhere, you go to the _____ area.

6. The _____ is the big building at the airport.

7. The _____ is a door where you get on the airplane.

8. Your _____ is a paper with your seat number.

C 🔁 Describe an experience at an airport. Use words from exercise **A**.

Grammar: Expressing prohibition

Expressing prohibition		
You	**must not** **can't**	bring a knife on the plane.

Must not and *can't* mean that something is not allowed. There is a law or rule against it.
*This meaning is different from *don't have to*.
  You **must not** *take pictures here.* = pictures are not allowed
  You **don't have to** *take pictures here.* = pictures are OK but not necessary

A Write sentences with *must*, *must not*, and *can't* about the signs on the right.

1. _____

2. _____

3. _____

4. _____

5. _____

B Complete the sentences about things to remember when going to the airport. Use your own ideas.

1. You have to _____.

2. You can't _____.

3. You must _____.

4. You don't have to _____.

Conversation

A 🔊 **20** Close your book and listen to the conversation. What time will the traveler get on the plane?

Check-in agent:	Good afternoon. Where are you flying to today?
Traveler:	To Caracas. Here's my ticket.
Check-in agent:	Thank you. Would you like a window seat or an aisle seat?
Traveler:	A window seat, please.
Check-in agent:	And do you have any bags to check?
Traveler:	Just one. And this is my carry-on bag.
Check-in agent:	OK. Here's your boarding pass. You're in seat 27A. Boarding time is 10:15, but you must be at the gate 15 minutes before that.
Traveler:	I have a question. Is there a restaurant after the security check?
Check-in agent:	Yes, there are two. Thank you, and enjoy your flight!

B 🔁 Practice the conversation with a partner. Switch roles and practice it again.

C 🔁 Make new conversations with this information.

1. Seoul | aisle seat | two bags | 15C | 2:30 pm | a place to buy a newspaper
2. London | window seat | two bags | 30E | 4:00 pm | a pharmacy

D 🔁 **GOAL CHECK** ✔ **Use English at the airport**

Pretend a partner is a foreigner at your local airport. Ask and answer questions about what you have to do to board your plane.

Reading

A 🔁 Discuss these questions with a partner.

1. Which places in your country get the most tourists?

2. Do the tourists cause any problems?

B Find the information in the text.

1. What did Khumbu look like 50 years ago?

   a. _____

   b. _____

2. What does much of Khumbu look like today? _____

3. What problems are caused by tourists in Khumbu?

   a. _____

   b. _____

   c. _____

   d. _____

4. What actions are people taking in Khumbu?

   a. _____

   b. _____

C Match the columns to complete the reasons.

1. Tourists visit Khumbu ___
   a. because it's too expensive.

2. More tourists go to Khumbu now ___
   b. because they want hot baths and foreign food.

3. The forests in Khumbu are gone ___
   c. because the wood was used for tourists.

4. Tourists use a lot of wood ___
   d. because the mountains are beautiful.

5. People don't burn kerosene ___
   e. because it's easy to get there.

Khumbu, Nepal

TOURISTS OR TREES?

Near Mount Everest, the highest mountain in the world, is a beautiful region of Nepal called Khumbu. Fifty years ago, it had thick forests, and the mountains were covered with red and pink flowers. Edmund Hillary and Tenzing Norgay started from Khumbu when they became the first people to climb Mount Everest in 1953.

Since then, thousands of visitors have come to Khumbu to enjoy the spectacular mountain scenery and to take an adventure vacation. Tourists hike between the villages and sleep in very small **guesthouses.**

guesthouses *small hotels, inns*   **trails** *paths for hiking*
deforestation *destruction of forests*   **kerosene** *fuel made from petroleum*

Now, however, much of Khumbu has become a desert, partly because over 25,000 tourists pass through every year. Most of them arrive by small plane from Kathmandu, the capital. In the past, the airport there was just a grassy field, but in 2000, a new terminal was built to allow planes and helicopters to bring in more visitors.

"We must reduce the number of tourists," says one local man. "They destroy the **trails** when they all walk in the same place. The guesthouses are crowded. People drop their water bottles and soda cans everywhere."

But the biggest problem of tourism is **deforestation.** Khumbu has lost most of its trees. They were cut down to build tea houses and to use for firewood.

"Tourists don't think about the problems they cause," says one scientist. "Especially about the wood that is used to cook their foreign food and heat water for their baths. One tourist uses as much wood in a day as five local families." Now local people have to walk many miles to find firewood.

One possible solution is to cook and heat water with **kerosene,** but it's too expensive for many local people. "The government has got to distribute kerosene to local people," says the scientist. "It's the only way to save the forest."

People in Nepal are taking action. One group has started a program to sell cheap kerosene. Another group, the Himalayan Trust started by Edmund Hillary, has planted more than a million trees in Khumbu. This will help to save the land and to produce wood products that people can sell. In 30 years, Khumbu may have forests and flowers again.

Climbers ascend through the Khumbu icefall on their way to the summit.

Grand Canal at night in Venice, Italy

What does tourism bring to Venice?
- money (shops, hotels, restaurants, etc.)
- energy and activity
- culture from other places

What does tourism bring to Venice?
- crowds, traffic, pollution
- higher prices (food, housing, etc.)
- rude behavior

The older person thinks tourism brings money to Venice. Tourists love to go shopping for souvenirs, and they stay in hotels, and . . .

Communication

A Look at each person's picture and opinion. Explain one person's viewpoint to your partner. Add details using your own ideas.

Writing

A In your notebook, list six places in the world that get a lot of tourism every year. Discuss why people like to visit these places.

B Brainstorm several positive and negative aspects of tourism to complete the t-chart below.

Tourism PROS (+)	Tourism CONS (−)

C How can tourists help a place they visit and not hurt it? In your notebook, write a paragraph with a topic sentence, three or more good ideas, and details about each idea.

D **GOAL CHECK** ✔ **Discuss the pros and cons of tourism**

Take turns. Read your paragraph to a small group of students. Discuss each other's opinions.

White-water rafting in New Zealand

Before You Watch

A Read about the video and check the meanings of the words in **bold**.

While You Watch

A ▶ Watch the video and circle **T** for *true* or **F** for *false*.

1. Queenstown is a beautiful and quiet place.   T   F
2. The jet boat was invented in New Zealand.   T   F
3. You can do sixty different activities in Queenstown.   T   F
4. Helicopter hikers stay on top of the mountain for a long time.   T   F
5. Everyone is happy after they try bungee jumping.   T   F

> The city of Queenstown in New Zealand is a world center for **adventure** sports. You can ride a fast jet boat through **shallow** water, go bungee jumping off a high **bridge**, or take a helicopter **hike** in the mountains. All of these **pastimes** give travelers a **thrill**. People call Queenstown "the adventure capital of the world."

B ▶ Watch the video again. Circle the correct answer.

1. The gap under the jump pod is (300 | 440) feet.
2. Jet boats were made to travel on (lakes | rivers).
3. The mountain hike takes (four | five) hours.
4. In helicopter hiking, people walk (up | down) the mountain.
5. The world's first bungee-jumping site was a (bridge | wire).

After You Watch / Communication

A Which of the activities in the video do you want to try? Why?

B 👥 Plan a three-day tour of your country for foreign visitors. What kind of tour will they have? Which places will they visit? What will they do there?

Careers

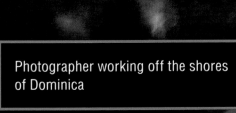

UNIT 11 GOALS

1. Discuss career choices

2. Ask and answer job-related questions

3. Talk about career planning

4. Talk about innovative jobs

Vocabulary

A 🔊 **21**   Listen to a conversation between a high school senior and a career advisor. What does Marcy do at the hospital?

B 🔊 **21**   Listen again. Then fill in the blanks in Ms. Carter's notes below with the words in the box.

> employee   experience   owner   assistant
> training   qualifications   volunteer   boss

- Marcy has some work _____. She went through a _____ program to become a family _____ at the hospital. It's _____ work, so Marcy doesn't get paid.

- Marcy would like to be a business _____, but she doesn't have the necessary _____ yet.

- I explained that she could start as an _____ at a business. Later, perhaps, she can be the _____ when she has her own business.

C 🔁   Talk in pairs. What do you think Marcy should do to prepare for her future? Did the advisor give her good advice?

Grammar: Modals for giving advice

Modals for giving advice	
Use modals of advice to talk about what is or isn't a good idea. Modals are followed by the simple form of a verb.	You **should** <u>choose</u> a career that fits your personality. Miguel **ought to** <u>become</u> an engineer. Linda **shouldn't** <u>take</u> that office job.
Had better is stronger than *should* or *ought to*. It means something bad could happen if the advice isn't followed.	You **had better** <u>talk</u> to the academic advisor before you decide on a major. I**'d better not** <u>miss</u> any more days of work.
Use *maybe, perhaps,* or *I think* with modals to make the advice sound gentler and friendlier.	**Maybe** you **should** <u>become</u> a health care worker.

A 🔄 Complete the sentences with a partner. Use your own ideas.

> **Career Advice**
>
> - If you want to become a successful businessperson, you should
>   _____ , but you shouldn't _____ .
>
> - If you really like animals, you ought to _____ .
>
> - When you go for a job interview, you had better _____ ,
>   and you had better not _____ . Good luck!

B 🔄 Read one of the problems out loud to a partner. Your partner will give you friendly advice using *maybe, perhaps*, or *I think*.

1. My school is far from my house.
2. I think I may be getting sick.
3. I want to become a doctor.
4. My job doesn't pay very well.
5. My university application was rejected.
6. I never remember my mother's birthday.

> I don't get along with my co-worker.

> Maybe you should avoid him.

Conversation

A 🔊 22 Close your book and listen to the conversation. Why doesn't Bob like his job?

Miranda: Hi Bob. How's it going?
Bob: Not so good. I think I need a new job.
Miranda: You do look stressed out. What is it you do again?
Bob: I'm an administrative assistant. That's like a secretary, but I have more responsibilities.
Miranda: Do you have a good boss?
Bob: Sure. He's the owner of the company, and he's pretty nice, actually.
Miranda: So what's the problem? Is it the other people you work with?
Bob: No, my co-workers are fine, but I do the same thing every day.
Miranda: Maybe you should start looking for a more interesting job.
Bob: You're right. I can probably find something better.

B 🔄 Practice the conversation with a partner. Then have new conversations about problems that might be nice to have; for example:

I make too much money.   **I have too much vacation time.**

C 🔄 **GOAL CHECK** ✔ **Discuss career choices**

Work in pairs. Choose a career from the box and describe the training, experience, and other qualifications required for that career. Then talk about the advantages and disadvantages of having that career.

> sales representative
> information technology specialist
> lawyer
> health care worker
> computer software engineer

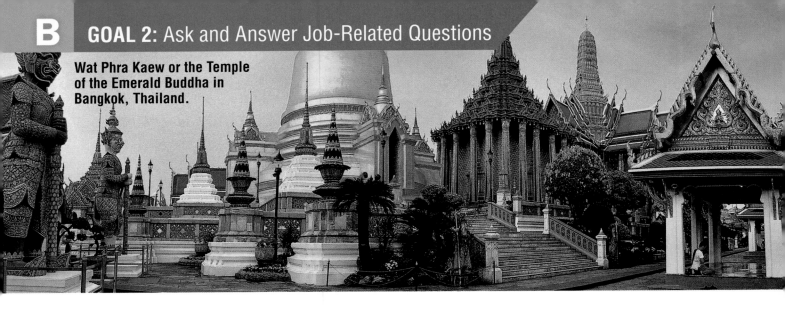

B **GOAL 2: Ask and Answer Job-Related Questions**

Wat Phra Kaew or the Temple of the Emerald Buddha in Bangkok, Thailand.

Engage!

Is it better to be a business owner or an employee?

Listening

A 🔊 **23** Listen to an interview with a restaurant owner. Why did he start his own business?

B 🔊 **23** Listen again and answer the questions.

1. When did Mr. Sangumram open the New Thailand restaurant? _____

2. Who is the cook at the restaurant? _____

3. What kind of food is served at the restaurant? _____

4. How far from the owner's home is the restaurant? _____

5. How many employees work at the restaurant? _____

6. What does Mr. Sangumram's wife do for a living? _____

C 🔁 What makes a good job? Rank the following from 1 (most important) to 6 (least important). Share your answers with a partner.

_____ amount of vacation time   _____ distance from home

_____ wage or salary level   _____ long-term employment

_____ working alone or with others   _____ interesting job duties

Pronunciation

In *yes/no* questions, the speaker's voice rises on the last content word.

Did you talk to your boss?   **Is she going to pay you a higher salary?**

In questions with *wh-* words, we use a rising then falling intonation over the last content word.

When is your job interview?   **What qualifications do you need?**

138   Unit 11

A 🔊 **24** Listen to the following questions. Then listen again and repeat.

Yes/No questions	*Wh-* questions
1. Do you like your co-workers?	6. When is the training?
2. Was your boss in a good mood?	7. How old do you have to be?
3. Is this part of the job?	8. Which company is better?
4. Did you learn any useful skills?	9. What time should I be here?
5. Are you making good progress?	10. How many employees are there?

B 🔄 Imagine you are applying for a job at Mr. Sangumram's restaurant. He needs a waiter, a dishwasher, and an assistant cook. Which job would you apply for? Write questions about the job with a partner.

Yes/No questions	*Wh-* questions
Is the restaurant open late at night?	What are the job duties?
_____	_____
_____	_____
_____	_____

C 👥 Join another pair of students and role-play a job interview. Ask the other pair your questions from exercise **B.** They will answer using their own ideas.

Communication

A Read the career profiles on the right. Choose two careers that might be good for you, but don't tell anyone which jobs you chose.

B 🔄 Ask your partner several questions about the kind of career he or she might want in the future. Then try to guess which two careers your partner chose.

> **Do you like to work outdoors?**

> **How much do you know about medications?**

C 👥 **GOAL CHECK** ✔ **Ask and answer job-related questions**

Join another pair of students. Ask each other questions and decide which career is best for each person in the group.

Career Profiles

Commercial Pilot:
Knows about airplane mechanics, weather, radio communication. Works long hours. Often far away from home.

Pharmacist:
Knows about medications. Advises patients about their treatments. Long-term employment. Some vacation time.

Diving Instructor:
Understands and teaches the use of scuba equipment. Works outdoors. Should be a strong swimmer. Salary varies by season.

Retail Sales Clerk:
Manages store merchandise. Assists customers. Should be able to work with others and stand for several hours at a time.

Language Expansion: Participial adjectives

A Read the article about A. J. Coston. What nouns do the words in blue describe?

> **That was relaxing. Now I feel relaxed.**

> **I think you went to a park.**

Word Focus

Participial Adjectives

That was _____ .
Now I feel _____ .

relaxing/relaxed
embarrassing/embarrassed
tiring/tired
confusing/confused
disappointing/disappointed
exciting/excited
depressing/depressed

A. J. Coston isn't waiting to start his dream job. At age 18, he's a weekend volunteer firefighter in the United States. During the week, he lives at home with his mom, dad, and sister, and does his main job: going to high school. "I always wanted to get into firefighting since I was a little kid watching fire trucks go by," he says. "One day I was bored and on the Internet, and I found out that Loudoun County offered a junior firefighter program."

Some of A. J.'s friends are surprised by his decision to spend weekends at the firehouse, but to A. J., helping people is more satisfying than anything else. The job is never boring, either, since firefighters get called to all sorts of emergencies. One terrifying moment for A. J. was getting an emergency call after four children were struck by lightning. Luckily, all four survived.

A. J. will be off to college next fall, and plans to study what he's most interested in: emergency medical care. "I want to be a flight medic on a helicopter eventually," he says.

B 🔁 For each participial adjective in blue above, decide whether it describes (1) someone's feelings or (2) something that causes a certain feeling. Then practice the sentences in the Word Focus box with a partner. Guess what might have happened.

Grammar: Indefinite pronouns

Pronouns refer to specified nouns (people, places, or things). Indefinite pronouns refer to unspecified nouns (people, places, or things).	I know <u>the career advisor</u>. **She** lives in my neighborhood. **Somebody** locked the door. *(I don't know who did it.)*
Use *everybody/everyone/everything* to talk about <u>all</u> of a group of nouns.	**Everything** in the book is important. You need to study all of it.
Use *nobody/no one/nothing* to talk about <u>none</u> of a group of nouns.	I want to sell my computer, but **no one** I know wants to buy it.
Use *somebody/someone/something* to talk about an unspecified noun.	You should talk to **someone** at the career counseling center.
Use *anybody/anyone/anything* to emphasize that it's not important to specify a certain person, place, or thing.	You need work experience. **Anything** you do will be helpful. *(It doesn't matter what it is.)*
Use *anybody/anyone/anything* in negative statements and in questions.	I don't know **anybody** at my school. Do you know **anyone** at your school?
Indefinite pronouns always take the singular form of a verb.	**Everyone** <u>has</u> useful skills and knowledge.

A Complete the sentences with the simple present form of the verb in parentheses.

1. Everybody in my family _____ (enjoy) eating ice cream.

2. The university is looking for someone who _____ (plan) to study nanotechnology.

3. Nothing _____ (be) more discouraging than doing a job you don't like.

4. Nobody really _____ (know) what will happen in the future.

B Take turns reading the situation to a partner. Discuss the choices and circle the correct word.

1. *There are 18 students in the class. One student wants to leave early.*
   (Somebody | Everybody) wants to leave early.

2. *You have never heard of the field of ethnobotany before.*
   I don't know (anything | something) about ethnobotany.

3. *None of your friends, acquaintances, or family members have a luxury car.*
   (Anyone | No one) I know has a luxury car.

4. *You want to learn to speak Japanese. You are looking for a tutor.*
   I need to find (somebody | everybody) who speaks Japanese.

Conversation

A 🔊 25 Listen to the conversation. What is the man planning to do?

Parker: What do you want to do when you finish school?
Kimberly: I'm not sure, but I want to do something interesting.
Parker: Of course! Everybody wants that, but you need to start planning.
Kimberly: OK, what are you planning to do when you finish school?
Parker: I'm planning to enroll in a training program. They teach you how to install custom car stereos.
Kimberly: You sound excited about that.
Parker: I am! You know I've always loved cars, and the program is only four months long, so I can get a job really soon.
Kimberly: That sounds great! I need to start thinking about my future, too.
Parker: Mmm hmm. That's what I said before.
Kimberly: And you're right, as usual.

B 🔄 Practice the conversation with a partner. Switch roles and practice it again. Make a new conversation using your own plans for the future.

C 🔄 **GOAL CHECK** ✓ **Talk about career planning**

Talk to a partner. What kind of career would be interesting and satisfying to you? What are you doing now to prepare for your future career?

Reading

A 🗨 What jobs do you think of as especially innovative? Look at the list below or come up with your own ideas. Share them with a partner.

salesclerk	lawyer	inventor
bus driver	designer	researcher
programmer	travel photographer	

B Read the article. Complete the sentences with the correct words in parentheses.

1. Pritchard got his idea for the water purifier when he was _____. (happy / angry)

2. Pritchard works _____. (at home / in a laboratory)

3. He believes that "old thinking" needs to _____. (continue / change)

4. Many people have to _____ their water before they drink it. (buy / boil)

5. Lifesaver water purifiers are very _____. (efficient / expensive)

C 🗨 List two problems that drinking unsafe water causes. Compare your answers with a partner. How does the water purifying bottle help?

TED Ideas worth spreading

Michael Pritchard Inventor, Problem Solver

MAKING FILTHY WATER DRINKABLE

Like many **innovators,** Michael Pritchard gets good ideas when he sees a problem that needs to be solved. The **inspiration** for his Lifesaver water **purifier** came after the Asian tsunami of 2004 and Hurricane Katrina, which hit New Orleans in 2005. After both disasters, it took days for the people who were affected to get safe drinking water. That was too long, in Pritchard's opinion. It made him very angry.

"Everyone deserves safe drinking water," Pritchard says. Working in his garage and his kitchen, he developed a design for a simple water purifier. It took 18 months and a number of failed prototypes before he successfully created the Lifesaver bottle.

Pritchard believes that "old thinking," the traditional way of responding to disasters by making people travel to get safe drinking water, needs to change. Instead, he "thinks differently," looking for solutions that are simple to use, close to home, and inexpensive to operate.

The water purifying bottle meets all three needs. It can remove **contaminants** from 6,000 liters of dirty water before its filter needs to be replaced. A larger system, in a jerry can, is able to filter 25,000 liters of water. That's enough water for a family of four to drink for three years. It only costs a half a cent a day to operate. Because Lifesaver systems only clean as much water as a person, family, or community needs every day, it is much more efficient than other water purification systems.

Water poverty is the **lack** of a clean, reliable supply of drinking water. An estimated 1.1 billion people are trapped in water poverty. When people have access to clean water, it means that there is less disease.

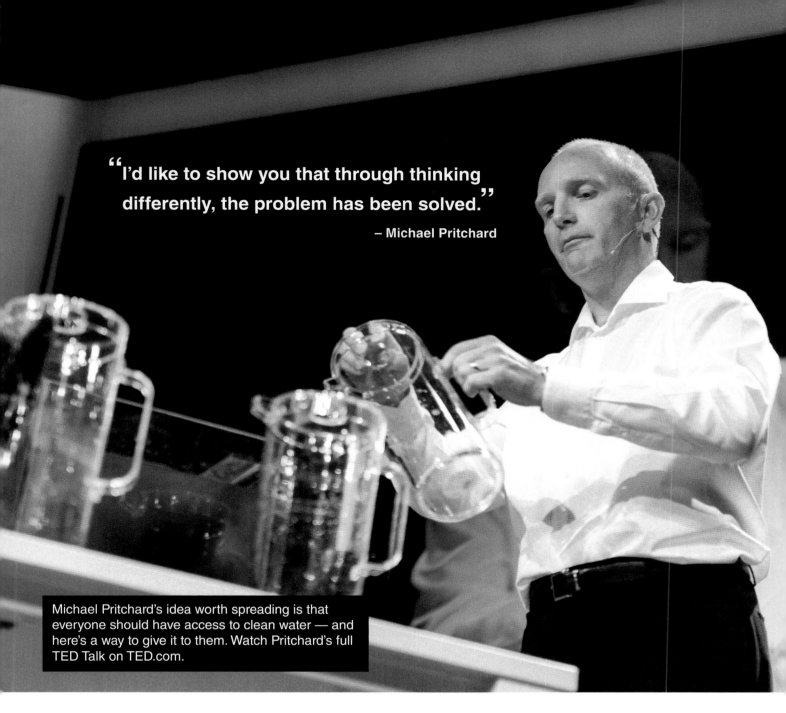

> **"I'd like to show you that through thinking differently, the problem has been solved."**
>
> – Michael Pritchard

Michael Pritchard's idea worth spreading is that everyone should have access to clean water — and here's a way to give it to them. Watch Pritchard's full TED Talk on TED.com.

They don't have to look for wood or use fossil fuels to boil their water before they drink it. It also means that many girls in developing countries, who are usually responsible for bringing clean water to their homes, can go to school instead. Lives are changed, lives are saved, and community life improves when people have reliable access to clean water.

Innovators like Michael Pritchard who think differently can make a big difference in the world.

innovator a person who creates something new to solve a problem

inspiration something that gives someone an idea about what to do or create

purifier a device used to remove harmful substances

contaminant something that makes a place or a substance unclean

lack the state of not having enough of something

▲ An employee shows a powerful new computer that will be able to handle the large amount of calculations needed for nano technology research

Writing

A Circle the correct indefinite pronouns to complete the sentences.

1. An inventor is (nobody | somebody) who is interested in problem solving.

2. Pritchard wanted to do (something | anything) to solve the problem of unsafe drinking water for millions of people around the world.

3. Pritchard did not work in a high-tech laboratory; he developed his innovation with almost (nothing | something).

4. (Everybody | Nobody) wants to make the world a better place.

5. I hope to do (something | anything) important with my life.

B Complete the letter with *should, shouldn't, had better*, or *ought to*.

I am happy you asked me for advice. If you want to become an innovator, you (1) _____ think about a problem you want to solve. Since there are lots of problems in the world, it (2) _____ be too hard! Remember, it takes a long time to solve a problem well, so you (3) _____ be patient.

community-based conservation

developing world

food systems

undersea exploration

endangered species

non-profit organization

Communication

A 🔁 What other innovators do you know? Look at the other TED readings and TED Talks. What makes them innovators? Use the ideas in the box.

B 🔾 **GOAL CHECK** ✔️ **Talk about innovative jobs**

Share your ideas about innovators. What do they have in common?

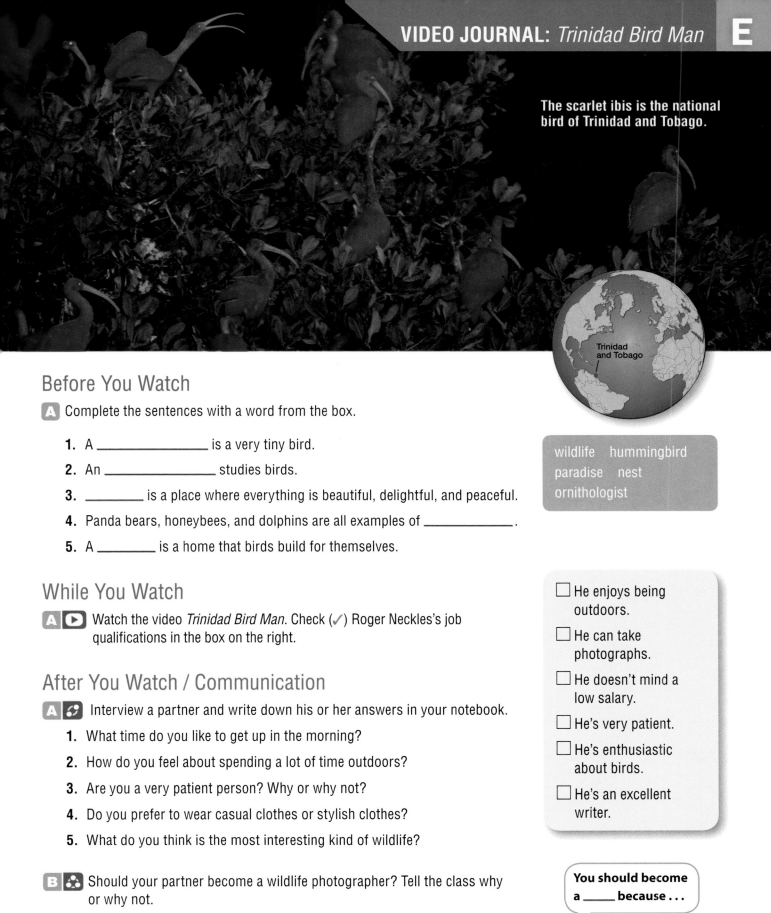

The scarlet ibis is the national bird of Trinidad and Tobago.

Trinidad and Tobago

Before You Watch

A Complete the sentences with a word from the box.

1. A _____ is a very tiny bird.
2. An _____ studies birds.
3. _____ is a place where everything is beautiful, delightful, and peaceful.
4. Panda bears, honeybees, and dolphins are all examples of _____.
5. A _____ is a home that birds build for themselves.

wildlife   hummingbird
paradise   nest
ornithologist

While You Watch

A ▶ Watch the video *Trinidad Bird Man*. Check (✓) Roger Neckles's job qualifications in the box on the right.

After You Watch / Communication

A 🔄 Interview a partner and write down his or her answers in your notebook.

1. What time do you like to get up in the morning?
2. How do you feel about spending a lot of time outdoors?
3. Are you a very patient person? Why or why not?
4. Do you prefer to wear casual clothes or stylish clothes?
5. What do you think is the most interesting kind of wildlife?

B 👥 Should your partner become a wildlife photographer? Tell the class why or why not.

☐ He enjoys being outdoors.
☐ He can take photographs.
☐ He doesn't mind a low salary.
☐ He's very patient.
☐ He's enthusiastic about birds.
☐ He's an excellent writer.

You should become a _____ because . . .

Celebrations

Carnival is celebrated in towns and villages throughout Brazil. Rio de Janeiro is the Carnival Capital of the World.

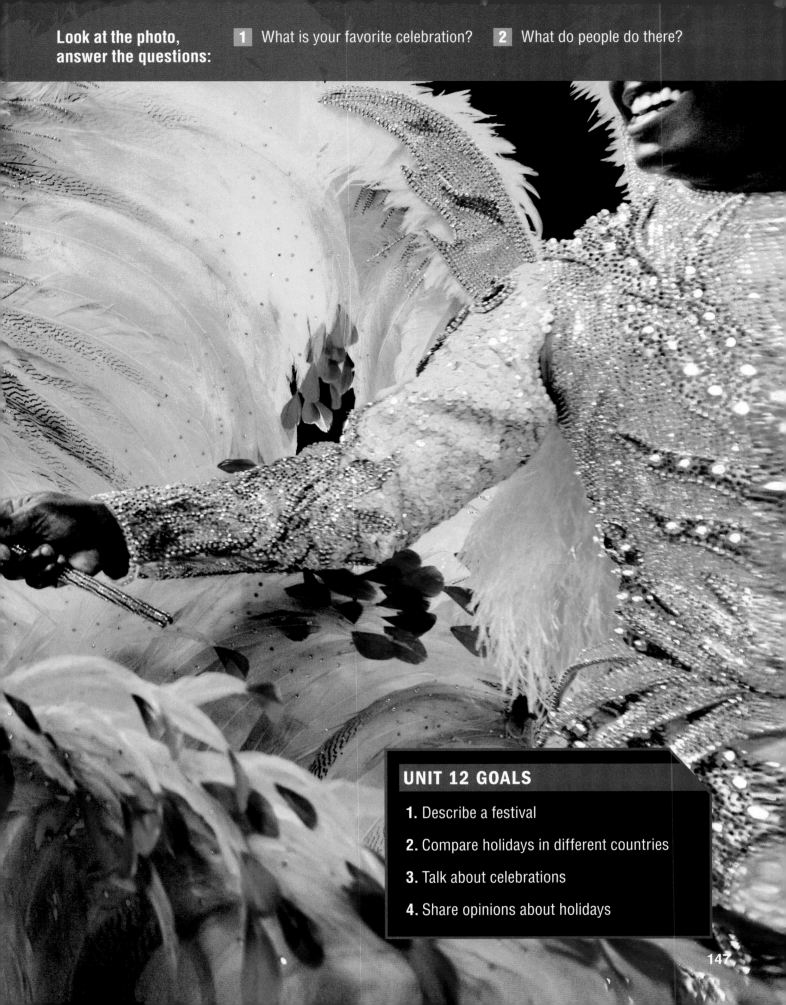

UNIT 12 GOALS

1. Describe a festival

2. Compare holidays in different countries

3. Talk about celebrations

4. Share opinions about holidays

▲ Hogmany celebration
in Scotland

Vocabulary

A Read about a special New Year's celebration.

New Year's Day is a holiday around the world, but people in Edinburgh, Scotland, celebrate it in an exciting way. They have a festival called Hogmanay. Hogmanay takes place all around the city, from December 29 to January 1. It starts with a parade on the night of December 29. On December 30, there are concerts and dancing. Finally, on New Year's Eve, there is a street party with fireworks, and people wear very colorful costumes. There is always a big crowd even though it's very cold. One year, more than 100,000 people participated. The celebration in Edinburgh is very well-known, but the annual Hogmanay festivals in other cities in Scotland are popular, too.

B Write the words in blue next to the correct meaning.

1. _____ delightful, thrilling

2. _____ happens

3. _____ famous

4. _____ a day when people don't work

5. _____ large group of people

6. _____ happening once each year

7. _____ special clothes for a performance

8. _____ an event with performances of music, etc.

9. _____ do something enjoyable for a special day

10. _____ took part in

C Discuss these questions with a partner. What festivals have you participated in? What festivals do you know about? Would you like to participate in Hogmanay in Edinburgh? Why or why not?

Engage!

How do you celebrate
New Year's Day?

Grammar: Comparisons with *as . . . as*

Subject + *be* +	*(not) as* + adjective + *as* +	complement
New Year's Day is	**as** exciting **as**	National Day. (The two holidays are equally exciting.)
Hogmanay is	**not as** popular **as**	Carnival. (Hogmanay is less popular than Carnival; Carnival is more popular than Hogmanay.)

*Use *as . . . as* to say that two things are equal. Use *not as . . . as* to say that two things are not equal.

A Look at the information about the two festivals. Write sentences with *(not) as . . . as*.

	The Spring Festival	The Harvest Fair
1. (old)	started in 1970	started in 1970
2. (long)	2 days	4 days
3. (popular)	5,000 people	5,000 people
4. (expensive)	tickets were $5	tickets were $20
5. (big)	10 concerts	23 concerts
6. (well-known)	on a few TV shows	on many TV shows

1. The Spring Festival _is as old as the Harvest Fair_ .
2. The Spring Festival _____ .
3. _____ .
4. _____ .
5. _____ .
6. _____ .

B 🔁 Choose two festivals or holidays. Make sentences with *as . . . as* comparing the celebrations.

> **Thanksgiving is as enjoyable as Christmas.**

> **Thanksgiving isn't as expensive as Christmas!**

Conversation

A 🔊 26 Close your book and listen to the conversation. When is the festival they talk about?

Dave: Yuki, are there any special festivals in your city?
Yuki: Oh, we have lots of festivals in Tokyo! My favorite is called *Setsubun*.
Dave: Really? What's that?
Yuki: Well, it takes place in February. We celebrate the last day of winter.
Dave: What do you do then?
Yuki: People throw special beans for good luck, and they say "Out with bad luck, in with good luck!" Then you eat one bean for each year of your age. And there are lots of parties.
Dave: That sounds like fun.
Yuki: It is!

B 🔁 Practice the conversation with a partner. Then have new conversations about your favorite holidays and celebrations.

C 🔁 **GOAL CHECK** ✔ **Describe a festival**

Talk to a partner about a special festival in your city. Tell your partner when, why, and how you celebrate this festival.

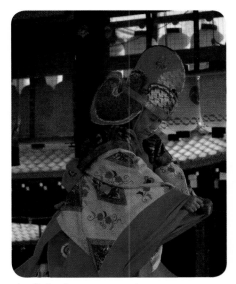

▲ Setsubun procession in Tokyo

GOAL 2: Compare Holidays in Different Countries

Day of the Dead

Country:

_____

When is it?

_____

How do people celebrate it?

a. go to the cemetery with

_____

b. bring

_____

What is the special food?

a. sweet

_____

b. shaped like skulls

_____

Listening

A ◀)) 27 Listen to three people talk about a holiday in their country. Number the countries in the order that you hear about them.

a. Japan _____   **b.** Mexico _____   **c.** United States _____

B ◀)) 27 Listen again and fill in the charts.

Halloween

Country: _____

When is it? _____

How do people celebrate it?

a. put on _____

b. ask for _____

c. watch _____

What is the special food?

a. _____

b. _____

O-Bon

Country: _____

When is it? _____

How do people celebrate it?

a. go back to _____

b. participate in a special _____

c. make big _____

C 🗨 Discuss these questions with a partner.

1. Do you know about any other holidays like this?

2. Why do you think different countries have similar holidays?

Pronunciation: Question intonation with lists

A 🔊 28 Listen to the questions. Notice how the intonation rises and falls in questions with a list of choices.

1. Would you like cake, ice cream, or fruit?

2. Is O-Bon in July or August?

B 🔊 29 Read the questions and mark the intonation with arrows. Then listen and check your answers.

1. Do you have special food at breakfast, lunch, or dinner?

2. Have you celebrated New Year's in France, Australia, or both?

3. Is your costume red or pink?

4. Is O-Bon in August or September?

5. Do you celebrate with dancing, singing, or gift-giving?

C 🗨 Say each question from exercise **B** to your partner. Give each other feedback on your pronunciation.

Communication

A 👥 Imagine that your group can take a trip to participate in one of the holidays in exercise **A** on page 150. Discuss these questions. Then explain your group's final decision to the class.

1. How are these holidays similar? Think of as many answers as you can.

2. How are they different?

3. What could visitors do at each holiday?

4. Which holiday would you like to participate in? Why?

B 🗨 **GOAL CHECK** ✔ Compare holidays in different countries

Take turns. Tell a partner how the different groups' trips will be similar and how they will be different.

C **GOAL 3:** Talk About Celebrations

Baseball team
celebrates after a win

Language Expansion: Expressions for celebrations

A Read the expressions and their functions.

Expressions and functions
• Congratulations! *(When someone is getting married, having a baby, getting a promotion, winning a game, etc.)* • Well-done! *(When someone has accomplished something difficult.)* • Thanks for having/inviting us! *(To thank someone after a party.)* • Good luck! *(To wish someone a good result or a good future.)* • Happy Birthday/Anniversary/New Year! etc. *(To greet someone on a holiday or special occasion.)*

B Write the correct expression for each situation.

1. You're leaving someone's house after a dinner party. _____

2. Your friend has to take a difficult exam tomorrow. _____

3. Your neighbor tells you he plans to get married soon. _____

4. Today is your friend's birthday. You see your friend. _____

5. Your friend got an excellent grade on an exam. _____

Grammar: *Would rather*

Use *would rather* + base form of the verb to talk about actions we prefer or like more than other actions.	**I would rather go** to a big wedding than go to a small wedding.
We often use a contraction of *would*.	**They'd rather meet** us at the library.
Use *would rather not* + base form of the verb to talk about things we don't want to do.	**She'd rather not go** to the meeting. It's going to be long and boring.
Use *would rather* + base form of the verb in *yes/no* questions to ask people about their preferences.	**Would you rather have** the dinner party at our house or at a restaurant?

152 Unit 12

A Write sentences about things you like to do on your birthday with *I'd rather*.

1. have (a big party/a small party) <u>I'd rather have a big party.</u>

2. eat (at home/in a restaurant) _____

3. invite (lots of people/a few close friends) _____

4. get (flowers/presents) _____

5. wear (nice clothes/jeans and a T-shirt) _____

6. (your own idea/your own idea) _____

B Ask your partner about his or her preferences. Use the choices in exercise **A** and *Would you rather . . . ?*

> **Would you rather have a big party or a small party?**

> **I'd rather have a big party!**

Conversation

A 🔊 30 Close your book and listen to the conversation. Which celebration is coming soon?

Mike: New Year's Eve is next week. What would you like to do?

Katie: Let's go to a party!

Mike: I'd rather just stay home and go to bed early.

Katie: That's boring! We could go out for dinner. Or would you rather go to a movie?

Mike: I'd rather not go out. It's always so noisy and crowded.

Katie: I have an idea. Let's cook a nice dinner at home and invite a few friends.

Mike: That sounds like a better plan.

B 🗣 Practice the conversation with a partner. Switch roles and practice it again.

C Make notes. What do you usually do to celebrate these days?

Your birthday	Your favorite holiday: _____

D 🗣 Work with a partner. Make plans to celebrate one of these days together.

E 👥 **GOAL CHECK** ✓ **Talk about celebrations**

Join another pair of students and share your plans.

Reading

A 🔄 Discuss these questions with a partner.

1. What are the most important holidays in your country?

2. Are they new or old? How did they start?

B Find this information in the reading.

1. the number of people who celebrate Kwanzaa now _____

2. the dates of Kwanzaa _____

3. the year when Kwanzaa started _____

4. the person who started Kwanzaa _____

   _____

5. three countries where people celebrate Kwanzaa _____

6. the most important symbol of Kwanzaa

   _____

7. the colors of Kwanzaa _____

C Circle **T** for *true*, **F** for *false*, or **NI** for *no information* (if the answer is not in the reading).

1. Kwanzaa is celebrated at the end of the year. **T F NI**

2. Kwanzaa is a holiday for African Americans. **T F NI**

3. Kwanzaa is a very old holiday. **T F NI**

4. People in Africa celebrate Kwanzaa. **T F NI**

5. People spend a lot of time with their families during Kwanzaa. **T F NI**

6. Children receive presents at the end of Kwanzaa. **T F NI**

7. Everyone thinks Kwanzaa is an important holiday. **T F NI**

STARTING A **NEW** TRADITION

Shantelle Davis is a nine-year-old girl in New York. On a cold night in December, her family is standing around the kitchen table while she lights a **candle.** The table is decorated with baskets of fruit and vegetables and **ears of corn** for Shantelle and her two brothers.

"This candle represents *umoja*, an African word that means being together," Shantelle says. "That's the most important thing for a family."

More than 5 million African Americans celebrate Kwanzaa every year from December 26 until January 1. It's a time when they get together with their families to think about their history and their ancestors in Africa.

Kwanzaa is very unusual because it was started by one man. In 1966, an American named Maulana Karenga wanted a holiday for African Americans to **honor** their culture and traditions. So he used words and customs from Africa to create a new celebration. He took the name Kwanzaa from the words for "first fruits" in Swahili, an African language. At first, only a few families had celebrations. Now, there are Kwanzaa events in schools and public places, and Kwanzaa has even spread to other countries, like Canada and Jamaica.

The main symbol of Kwanzaa is a **candleholder** with seven candles, one for each of the principles of Kwanzaa. Each night, a family member lights one of the candles and talks about the idea it represents: being together, being yourself, helping each other, sharing, having a goal, creating, and believing. The candles are red, black, and green, the colors of Kwanzaa. The parents also **pour** drinks to honor family members who have died. On the last night of Kwanzaa, there is a big dinner with African food, and children receive small presents.

Today, people can buy Kwanzaa greeting cards and special Kwanzaa clothes. Stores sell Kwanzaa candles and candleholders. Some people don't believe that Kwanzaa is as important as other holidays because it's so new. But other people say that Kwanzaa shows what is important in people's lives.

candle *stick of hard wax burned to provide light*
ear of corn *part of the corn plant* **honor** *show great respect for someone* **candleholder** *device to hold a candle*
pour *make a liquid flow into a container*

Chuseok celebration in Korea

Communication

I agree.
I'm not sure.
I disagree.

A Write your opinion about these sentences in your notebook. Use the expressions in the box.

1. A new holiday isn't a real holiday.

2. Some old holidays are not very important now.

3. Our country should start a new holiday.

4. People spend too much money for holidays.

5. It's very important to keep all of the old holiday customs.

B Compare your opinions with the opinions of other students. Talk about things your family does to celebrate holidays.

Writing

A Read the information about writing an opinion paragraph.

B Choose one of the statements from exercise **A** and write a paragraph about your opinion. Be sure the paragraph contains all three elements from the writing strategy.

C **GOAL CHECK** ✓ **Share opinions about holidays**

Read your partner's paragraph and write answers to the questions. Then explain your answers to your partner.

1. Does the paragraph have a strong, clear topic sentence? Explain.

2. Is your partner's opinion supported with good reasons? Explain.

3. Is there a conclusion that ends the paragraph well? Explain.

**Writing strategy:
An effective opinion paragraph**

1. Begin with a strong topic sentence which clearly states your point of view.

2. Support your opinion by giving good, logical reasons for it.

3. End with a brief conclusion related to the opinion and reasons you gave.

Young Mongolian riders going to the Naadam Festival.

Mongolia

Before You Watch

A 🔄 Discuss these questions with a partner. What do you know about Mongolia? Have you ever seen a horse race? Describe what you saw.

While You Watch

A ▶ Watch the video *Young Riders of Mongolia*. Write two unusual things about the Naadam horse race.

1. _____ 2. _____

B ▶ Watch the video again. Circle **T** for *true* or **F** for *false*.

1. In Mongolia today, people ride horses only for special celebrations. **T** **F**

2. The Naadam Festival celebrates traditional sports. **T** **F**

3. The Naadam horse race is very short. **T** **F**

4. People want to get close to the horses for good luck. **T** **F**

5. The winning horses get a lot of money. **T** **F**

After You Watch / Communication

A 👥 Discuss these questions in a small group. What are some traditional sports in your country? Are they still popular?

B 👥 Create a festival to introduce foreigners to the culture of your country. Present your festival to the class.

- Give the festival a name.

- Think of three sports, foods, and shows that will be in the festival.

- Make a poster to advertise your festival.

Before You Watch

A 🔁 **Look at the picture and answer the questions with a partner.**

1. Where are these people?
2. Why are they there?
3. What do you think they're doing?

B Sylvia Earle is one of the explorers in the picture. Here are some words you will hear in her TED Talk. Complete the paragraph with the correct word. Not all words will be used.

> **assets** *n.* valuable people or things
> **cope** *v.* to deal with problems and difficult situations and try to come up with solutions
> **depletion** *n.* reduction, shortage
> **drawn down** *v.* reduced
> **enduring** *adj.* continuing to exist in the same state or condition
> **impact** *n.* a powerful or major influence or effect
> **resilient** *adj.* able to become strong, healthy, or successful again after something bad happens

Dr. Sylvia Earle has been exploring Earth's oceans for more than 50 years. She knows how important it is to protect the (1) _____ that are found in the sea. She is worried about

> Sylvia Earle's idea worth spreading is that we need to do a better job of looking after our oceans, the world's "life support system." Watch Earle's full **TED**Talk on TED.com.

the (2) _____ of sea life she has seen—90% of the world's big fish are gone, (3) _____ by a growing population, pollution, and wasteful fishing practices. Dr. Earle believes that we must all work together to (4) _____ with this problem by reducing our (5) _____ on the ocean before it is too late.

C Look at the pictures on the next page. Check (✓) the information that you predict you will hear in the TED Talk.

_____ 1. The deep ocean is a dangerous place for humans.

_____ 2. When we know more about creatures that live in the sea, we can protect them better.

_____ 3. Human activity has changed the ocean in many negative ways.

While You Watch

A ▶ Watch the TED Talk. Circle the main idea.

1. If we don't protect the ocean, humans will be in danger, too.
2. There are many kinds of fish in the ocean that we don't know about.
3. It is important to develop new ways to catch fish.

> " . . . Nothing else will matter if we fail to protect the ocean. Our fate and the ocean's are one."
>
> – Sylvia Earle

B ▶ Look at the photos. Watch the TED Talk again and write the letter of the caption under the correct photo.

a. Sylvia Earle has developed many devices for underwater exploration.

b. There are many amazing creatures in the ocean.

c. Polar ice is shrinking, and life for polar bears is getting harder.

d. Sylvia Earle loves the ocean and all the creatures that live in it.

1. ___

2. ___

3. ___

4. ___

Challenge! 🔁 How would you describe Dr. Sylvia Earle's work as an ocean explorer? Is her work difficult or easy? Why does she do it? Talk to a partner about Sylvia Earle's career.

Sylvia Earle Oceanographer, National Geographic
Explorer-in-Residence

MY WISH—PROTECT OUR OCEANS

After You Watch

A Complete the summary with the words in the box.

ocean	protect
support	survival
trouble	understand

Sylvia Earle is worried about the (1) _____. Even more, she
is worried about our planet's (2) _____. The ocean is our life
(3) _____ system, and if we don't protect it, we will be in
(4) _____. Dr. Earle wants us to (5) _____ the ocean
and its creatures better, because if we understand the seas better, we will
want to (6) _____ them.

B Match the phrases to the information from the TED Talk.

_____ **1.** percent of the world's oceans that is protected   **a.** 50

_____ **2.** years that Sylvia Earle has been exploring the ocean   **b.** 90

_____ **3.** percent of life on the planet that lives in the ocean   **c.** 10

_____ **4.** percent of large fish species that have disappeared   **d.** 97

_____ **5.** number of years we have to protect the ocean   **e.** .08

C Read the statements below. Circle the ones that paraphrase Sylvia Earle's
ideas in the video.

1. The loss of fish species in the last 50 years is a problem.

2. People should use the ocean's resources any way they want to.

3. The oceans make it possible for human beings to live on earth.

4. The creatures that live in the deep ocean aren't as important as those
on land.

5. We only have a short time to protect the ocean.

One reason for the depletion of ocean resources is wasteful fishing practices.

Project

Sylvia Earle says that if we don't work to protect the oceans right now, we risk all life on the planet. She works with other scientists and explorers to find ways to protect and sustain ocean environments. What can be done to keep the ocean healthy for future generations?

A Look at these ways we can work to protect the ocean. Which ones are the most urgent? Rank them from most urgent (1) to less urgent (6).

_____ recycle plastics so they don't end up in the ocean

_____ change the way fishermen work so that less fish is wasted

_____ keep oil and other toxic chemicals out of the sea

_____ use less energy (gasoline and electricity) to slow global warming

_____ share the message that protecting the ocean is our collective responsibility

_____ establish conservation/protection zones

B Compare your rankings in exercise **A** with a partner. Do you have the same priorities? Think of some other ways to protect the ocean.

C Use Sylvia Earle's ideas to write a paragraph about ways we can help keep the ocean safe for future generations. Then show your paragraph to a different partner. Are your ideas well organized?

> The oceans are in danger, and everyone can help to save them. If we
> want to _____ , we should start with _____ .
> By doing _____ , we can. It is also important to change
> _____ . Finally, we need to _____ .

Challenge! Dr. Sylvia Earle has a really big idea worth spreading—one that can change the world and save our oceans. Research what your country's experts are doing to protect oceans and other aquatic environments. Share your ideas with the class.

Research Strategy

Using the search function on web pages

If you want to learn more about a topic on a Web site, use the Web site's search function. You can usually find search windows at the top of the page. They are usually located next to a magnifying glass icon. Sometimes search results can be sorted by relevance, date of publication, or type of resource.

GLOSSARY

UNIT 1

beans: a legume plant whose seeds sometimes are different colors, such as black or red, and can be cooked and eaten

climate: normal weather patterns

coast: describes an area near the ocean

corn: a grain that is grown on tall green plants and usually has large yellow seeds that are fed to animals or cooked and eaten by people

crop: a kind of plant grown for food

delicious: something that is good-tasting

disgusting: something that causes great dislike

farmer: person who produces food

flat: describes an area without mountains

fragrant: something that has a pleasant or perfumed smell

geography: the study of the surface of the earth

humid: describes air that is moist

land: areas of earth's upper crust composed mainly of soil and sometimes bodies of fresh water, such as rivers or lakes

lentils: a legume plants whose small round seeds can be cooked and eaten

meal: breakfast, lunch, and dinner

mountain: a tall formation of land and rock higher than a hill

oats: a type of grain usually eaten by animals and people

potatoes: a round starchy root vegetable that can be cooked and eaten

rice: a grain used for food that is usually small and white and grows in watery areas

region: a large area

smelly: something that has a strong or unpleasant smell

soybeans: a legume plant native to Asia, used to make foods such as tofu and soy sauce

staple food: very important food

wheat: a grain usually ground into flour and used to make things such as pasta or bread

yams: a plant with an orange root that can be cooked and eaten, sometimes called sweet potato

yucca: a plant, usually grown in warm climates, whose root can be cooked and eaten

UNIT 2

connect: bring together

culture: people with the same language and way of living

custom: an activity that is usual in a country

formal: very serious and important

gesture: a body movement to show something (a feeling, an idea, etc.)

greeting: the first words or actions used upon meeting someone

informal: friendly and relaxed

misunderstanding: a mistaken idea that causes confusion

rule: the correct way to do something

small talk: conversation about things that aren't important

smile: turn one's lips up at the corners, usually to show good feelings

traditional: the same for a long time without changing

UNIT 3

commute: travel to your job

crowded: too full

east: the direction where the sun comes up—usually at the right of a map

highway: a road where cars go fast

key: (on a map) the section of a map that explains the meaning of the symbols

neighborhood: one area in a city

nightlife: things to do in the evening

noisy: too loud

north: the direction that's usually at the top of a map

population: the number of people who live in a place

public transportation: trains, buses, and subways

rural: in the country

scale: (on a map) the section of a map that explains the distances

south: the direction that's usually at the bottom of a map

traffic: cars moving on a street

urban: in the city

west: the direction where the sun goes down—usually at the left of a map

UNIT 4

artery: one of the large blood vessels going from the heart

bone: a hard, white part of the body that makes up its frame (the skeleton)

brain: the organ in the head used for thinking and feeling

fever: higher than normal body temperature

headache: a pain in your head

heart: the organ in the chest that pumps blood through the body

hiccup: a sharp sound you make in your throat

indigestion: pain in the stomach because of something you have eaten

insomnia: not able to sleep

large intestine: the lower part of the tube in the body that carries food away from the stomach

liver: the organ in the body that helps in making sugar for energy and in cleaning the blood

lung: one of two breathing organs in the chest that supply oxygen to the blood

muscle: a part of the body that connects the bones and makes the body move

nausea: a feeling like you are going to vomit

pimple: a small red swelling on the skin

skin: the outer covering of the body

small intestine: the upper part of the tube in the body that carries food away from the stomach

sore throat: a general feeling of pain in the throat

stomach: the internal body part where food goes after being swallowed

vein: any of the tubes that bring blood to the heart and lungs

UNIT 5

achieve: succeed in making something happen

adventure: something unusual and exciting

amazing: very surprising and wonderful

artist: a person who creates art such as a painter or a musician

break down: something that stops working

business person: someone who works in the business world

challenge: something that is new and difficult to do

equipment: things you need for a particular purpose

explorer: a person who explores unfamiliar areas, an adventurer

give up: stop trying

goal: something you hope to be able to do through your efforts over time

grow up: grow from a child to an adult

keep on: continue trying

mental: something that is related to the mind

political figure: someone who works in a political field, such as a governor, mayor, or president

physical: something that is related to the body

progress: an advancement towards a goal

put up with: accept something bad without being upset

run out of: finish the amount of something that you have

scientist: a person who works and conducts research within the field of science

set out: leave on a trip

skill: an activity that needs special knowledge and practice

watch out: be very careful

writer: a person who makes a living by writing

UNIT 6

adolescence: the part of life when you are becoming an adult

adult: a person aged 20 or over

adulthood: the part of life when you are an adult

baby: a person aged 0–1

child: a person aged 2–12

childhood: the part of life when you are a child

childish: describes a person who is older, but acting like a child (bad)

elderly: describes a person who looks and acts old

in his/her twenties: describes a person who is between 20 and 29 (also **in his teens, thirties, forties,** etc.)

infancy: the part of life when you are a baby

mature: describes a person who is old enough to be responsible and make good decisions

middle-aged: describes a person who is not young or old (about 40–60)

old age: the part of life when you are old

retired: describes a person who has stopped working in old age

senior citizen: an old person (polite term)

teenager: a person aged 13–19

youthful: describes a person who is older, but with the energy of a young person (good)

UNIT 7

build: to make something from different parts or materials

diamond: the hardest gemstone, made of colorless carbon and very valuable

electronics: machines that use electricity such as laptops, televisions, or musical equipment

emerald: a precious green gemstone

expensive watch: a highly-priced small clock worn around the wrist

fame: the state of being well-known and talked about

find: to come across or chance upon something

freeze: to preserve food by keeping it very cold

fur coat: a coat made from the hairy skin of an animal

give: to offer something freely, to make a gift

gold: a precious yellow metal used to make jewelry, coins, and other objects

handmade jewelry: decorative items, crafted by artisans, that people wear such as rings, bracelets, and necklaces

know: to posses knowledge or understand something

lose: to become unable to find

luxury: great comfort at great expense

pearl necklace: a string of smooth, round, white objects, formed naturally in oysters, that is worn around the neck

precious metals: extremely valuable, costly metals such as gold

precious stones: extremely valuable, costly stones such as diamonds

put: to place something

send: to cause to go or move

silk shirt: the material made by silkworms sewn into a piece of clothing worn on the upper body, usually with sleeves, a collar, and buttons

silver: a white, shinny, metallic element used for making jewelry, knives, forks, spoons, and other objects

UNIT 8

badly: the adverb form of *bad*

beautifully: the adverb form of *beautiful*

extinct: doesn't exist any more, all dead

fast: the adverb form of *fast*

habitat: the place where an animal usually lives

hunt: to look for animals and kill them

loudly: the adverb form of *loud*

predator: an animal that kills other animals

prey: an animal that other animals kill to eat

protect: to keep safe from danger

slowly: the adverb form of *slow*

species: a kind of animal

well: the adverb form of *good*

wild: in nature, not controlled by people

UNIT 9

bring back: to take something back from where it was taken

bring up: raise someone and care for until fully grown

beyond: on the other side of

despite: even though, in spite of

distant: far away

exchange: a trade, transaction of ideas or objects

figure out: work through a problem to find a solution

give up: stop doing or having something

help out: do something good for someone

inspired: to motivate or stimulate

published: to print and distribute to the public

put on: (clothing) to dress

remarkable: something that is worthy of attention, extraordinary or outstanding

search: the action of looking for something

ships: large boats used to navigate large bodies of water

trade: an exchange of objects or materials for financial gain

turn on: use a switch to turn on an electrical appliance or machine

UNIT 10

airline agent: a person who works for an airline at an airport

baggage claim: the part of an airport where travelers get their bags back

boarding pass: a card that shows your seat number on an airplane

carry-on bag: a small bag that you can take on an airplane with you

departures: the part of an airport where travelers leave

gate: the part of an airport where travelers get on an airplane

itinerary: a plan for where you will go on a trip

passport: an official document that you must show when you enter or leave a country

reservation: a place that is saved for you in a hotel, airplane, train, etc.

security check: the part of an airport where officers look for dangerous things in travelers' bags

sightseeing: the act of visiting special places as a tourist

terminal: a large building at an airport

ticket: a printed piece of paper that says you paid for a place on a train, airplane, etc.

travel agent: a worker who arranges trips for other people

vaccination: an injection that stops you from getting a particular disease

visa: a stamp or paper that allows you to enter a foreign country

UNIT 11

assistant: someone who helps another person do their work; a word used before job titles to indicate slightly lower rank

bored: a feeling of being uninterested in something

boring: uninteresting

boss: the person in charge of others

computer software engineer: someone who designs computer programs

employee: someone who works for a person, business, or government

experience: understanding gained through doing something

health care worker: someone who gives medical care

information technology specialist: an expert in the theory and practice of using computers to store and analyze information

interested: a feeling of curiosity or a desire to know more about a subject

lawyer: a professional who practices law

owner: someone with a business that belongs to him or her

qualification: an ability that makes someone suitable to do something

sales representative: someone who sells goods and services, usually outside of a store

satisfying: something that meets your wants or needs

surprised: a feeling of pleasure or shock over an unexpected event

terrifying: causing a strong fear in someone

training: a process of education, instruction

volunteer: someone who agrees to do something because they want to, not because they have to

UNIT 12

annual: every year

celebrate: do something enjoyable for a special day

Congratulations!: a greeting you use when someone graduates or gets a new job

costume: special clothes that people wear for a performance or for a holiday

crowd: a very large group of people in one place

exciting: makes you feel happy and enthusiastic

festival: a time with many performances of music, dance, etc.

Good luck!: a greeting used to wish someone a good result

Happy anniversary!: a greeting you use when people celebrate being married for a certain number of years (such as 10, 25, or 50)

Happy birthday!: a greeting you use when someone has a birthday

Happy New Year!: a greeting you use on New Year's Day

holiday: a day when people don't work

participate: take part in

take place: happen

Thanks for having/inviting us!: a greeting used to thank someone for inviting you to their home or party

Well-done!: a greeting used to congratulate someone when they accomplish something difficult

well-known: famous

SKILLS INDEX

GRAMMAR

as + adjective + *as*, 148–149
active voice, 84–84
adjectives
    for age, 72
    comparatives, 44–45
    equatives, 44–45, 136–137
    with *how*, 72–73
    participial, 140
    superlatives, 44–45
adverbs
    already/ever/never/yet, 20–21
    enough/not enough/too + adjective, 60–61
    with *how*, 72–73
    of manner, 100
equatives, 44–45, 136–137
how + adjective or adverb, 72–73
indefinite pronouns, 140–141
infinitives of purpose, 49
modals
    for giving advice, 136–137
    of necessity, 124–125
    of prohibition, 128–129
passive voice, 84–85, 88–89
quantifiers, 100–101
real conditionals in future, 96–97
used to, 108–109
verbs
    future with *will*, 28–29
    irregular, 88
    passive voice with *by*, 88–89
    past continuous vs. simple past, 56
    past continuous with the simple past, 57
    past passive voice, 112–113
    phrasal verbs, 60, 112
    present passive voice, 84–85
    present perfect tense, 16–17, 20–21, 68–69
    simple past tense, 8–9
    simple present vs. present continuous tense, 4–5
    will + time clauses, 32–33
would rather, 152–153

LISTENING

conversations, 9, 18, 21, 33, 49, 61, 73, 89, 101, 113, 129, 141, 153
discussions, 46, 86, 126, 150
interviews, 6, 58, 138
radio programs, 30, 70, 98
talk, 110

PRONUNCIATION

content words, 86
-ed endings, 59
emphatic stress, 30
function words, 86
have/has vs. contractions, 18
intonation in questions, 138–139, 151
linking with
    comparatives and superlatives, 47
    final consonant followed by vowel, 7
phrases in sentences, 99
reductions
    got to/have to/has to, 126–127
    used to, 111
schwa (ə), 70
sentence stress, 86–87

READING SKILLS, 10, 22, 34, 50, 62, 74, 90, 102, 114, 130, 142, 154

READINGS

A Slice of History, 10–11
Arctic Dreams and Nightmares, 62–63
How Food Shapes Our Cities, 34–35
How Poachers Became Caretakers, 102–103
Living Beyond Limits, 74–75
Lord of the Mongols, 114–115
Making Filthy Water Drinkable, 142–143
Perfume: the Essence of Illusion, 90–91
Starting a New Tradition, 154–155
Taking Pictures of the World, 22–23
Tiny Invaders, 50–51
Tourists or Trees?, 130–131

SPEAKING

asking and answering questions, 5, 9, 17, 45, 57, 139
comparing, 4–5
conversations, 5, 7, 9, 17, 19, 21, 29, 31, 33, 45, 49, 57, 61, 69, 71, 73, 85, 89, 97, 109, 111, 137, 141, 149, 153
describing, 9,
discussing, 11, 17, 98,
explaining, 31
ice breakers, 20–21
making plans, 33
role playing, 49, 99
small talk, 18–21
suggesting, 49, 91

TEST-TAKING SKILLS

checking off answers, 29, 34, 44, 59, 65, 74, 102, 110, 114, 145
circling answers, 6, 18, 19, 25, 28, 30, 32, 37, 38, 40, 41, 58, 60, 62, 65, 70, 74, 76, 78, 80, 81, 93, 98, 101, 118, 120, 124, 133, 141, 144, 158, 160
completing charts, 6, 31, 41, 71, 81, 84, 87, 101, 121, 132, 153

definitions, 4, 16, 28, 48, 148

filling in blanks, 4, 5, 9, 10, 16, 21, 44, 56, 57, 62, 109, 128, 133, 145

labeling pictures, 32, 39, 46, 68, 79, 84, 119, 124, 159

list making, 10, 13, 24, 31, 33, 37, 47, 50, 59, 84, 90, 102, 125, 127, 132, 142

matching, 13, 34, 39, 40, 49, 53, 60, 79, 80, 85, 86, 93, 96, 119, 120, 130, 159, 160

multiple choice, 6, 10, 18, 30, 58, 62

ranking answers, 36, 138, 161

sentence completion, 5, 9, 10, 17, 21, 24, 29, 36, 38, 40, 45, 57, 61, 69, 73, 78, 80, 85, 97, 98, 100, 104, 109, 111, 113, 118, 120, 128, 137, 141, 142, 144, 145, 158, 160

true or false, 8, 22, 37, 50, 53, 74, 93, 110, 114, 117, 133, 154, 157

underlining answers, 7, 47, 49, 87

unscrambling sentences, 73

TOPICS

Careers, 134–145

Celebrations, 146–157

Challenges, 54–65

Cities, 26–37

Express Yourself, 14–25

Food from the Earth, 2–13

Life in the Past, 106–117

Luxuries, 82–93

Nature, 94–105

The Body, 42–53

Transitions, 66–77

Travel, 122–133

VIDEO JOURNALS

Adventure Capital of the World, 133

Coober Pedy Opals, 93

Fes, 37

Forbidden Fruit, 13

Happy Elephants, 105

Nubian Wedding, 77

Orangutan Language, 25

Searching for Genghis Khan, 117

Searching for the Snow Leopard, 65

The Human Body, 53

Trinidad Bird Man, 145

Young Riders of Mongolia, 157

VOCABULARY

adjectives for age, 72

adverbs of manner, 100

ailments, 48

animals and nature, 96

body parts, 44

careers, 136

challenges, 56

communication: culture and gestures, 16

festivals and holidays, 148

food staples, 8

geography and climate, 4

geographical locations, 32

greetings for celebrations, 152

ice breakers, 20

irregular verbs, 88

life in the past, 108

life stages, 68, 72

luxury items, 84

maps, 32

participial adjectives, 140

phrasal verbs, 60, 112

travel, 124, 128

urban life, 28

WRITING

advertisements, 92

emails, 12

letters, 52, 144

list-making, 36, 132

opinions, 24, 156

paragraphs, 24, 64, 76, 104, 116, 132, 156

predictions, 36

ILLUSTRATION:

8: (tl) Kenneth Batelman; **32:** (t) Kenneth Batelman; **44:** (t, c, b) Sharon & Joel Harris/IllustrationOnline.com; **48:** (1,2,3,4,5) Keith Neely/IllustrationOnline.com; **93, 98, 110:** (inset) National Geographic Maps; **124:** (1,2,4,5,6,7,8) Patrick Gnan/IllustrationOnline.com; **124:** (3) Ralph Voltz/IllustrationOnline.com; **128:** (t) Ralph Voltz/IllustrationOnline.com; **129:** (1,2,3,4,5) Nesbitt Graphics, Inc.; **145:** (inset) National Geographic Maps.

PHOTO:

Cover Photo: ©Jörg Dickmann

2–3: (f) Lannen/Kelly Photo/Alamy; **4:** (t) coolbiere photograph/Getty Images; **5:** (r) KRISTA ROSSOW/National Geographic Creative; **6:** (t) FRANS LANTING/National Geographic Creative; **7:** (t) Farrell Grehan/CORBIS; **9:** (b) foodfolio/Alamy; **11:** (t) © Dan DeLong Photography; **11:** (t) Rusty Hill/Photolibrary/Getty Images; **12:** (t) enviromantic/Getty Images; **13:** (t) IRA BLOCK/National Geographic Creative; **13:** (b) isarescheewin/Thinkstock; **14–15:** (f) Monty Rakusen/Cultura/Aurora Photos; **16:** (t) CORY RICHARDS/National Geographic Creative; **17:** (b) Roc Canals Photography/Getty Images; **18:** (t) Purestock/Alamy; **19:** (b) Fuse/Thinkstock; **20:** (t) © iStockphoto.com/gremlin; **21:** (b) MIKE THEISS/National Geographic Creative; **22–23:** (f) Courtesy of Annie Griffiths; **23:** (t) Annie Griffiths/National Geographic Creative; **24:** (t) Annie Griffiths/National Geographic Creative; **25:** (t) Michael Nichols/National Geographic Creative; **25:** (b) FRANS LANTING/National Geographic Creative; **26–27:** (f) watchlooksee.com/Getty Images; **28:** (t) Mike Theiss/National Geographic Creative; **29:** (b) Sean Pavone/Alamy; **30:** (t) Amy Toensing/National Geographic Creative; **31:** (t) © iStockphoto.com/Plougmann; **33:** (b) Kevin Kozicki/Thinkstock; **35:** (c) TED/James Duncan Davidson; **36:** (t) Louis-Laurent Grandadam/The Image Bank/Getty Images; **37:** (t) Juan Carlos Munoz/Age Fotostock; **37:** (b) Hemis/Alamy; **38:** (t) ©

Kate Vokovich; **39:** (t, bl, bcl, bcr, br) TED; **40, 41:** (t) TED; **42–43:** (f) Cory Richards/National Geographic Creative; **45:** (t) Dirima/Thinkstock; **46:** (t) Ingram Publishing/Thinkstock; **46:** (t) Purestock/Thinkstock; **46:** (t) Maksim Shmeljov/Thinkstock; **47:** (r) Pilin_Petunyia/Thinkstock; **48:** (t) Marion C. Haßold/Getty Images; **49:** (b) Alex Mares-Manton/Getty Images; **50:** (m) Kim Kwangshin/Science Source; **50–51:** (f) xrender/Thinkstock; **52:** (t) KidStock/Getty Images; **53:** (t) Tara Moore/Getty Images; **53:** (r) © Sebastian Kaulitzki/Shutterstock.com; **54–55:** (f) © Donald Miralle; **56:** (t) GEORGE F. MOBLEY/National Geographic Creative; **57:** (r) Daniel Milchev/Getty Images; **58:** (l) © Nav Dayanand; **58:** (t) FRITZ HOFFMANN/National Geographic Creative; **58:** (r) Suttiporn Suksumek/Thinkstock; **58:** (t) John Cancalosi/Getty Images; **58:** (r) Joel Sartore/National Geographic Creative; **60:** (t) James A. Sugar/National Geographic Creative; **61:** (r) Valeriya Repina/Thinkstock; **62–63:** (f) Sebastian Devenish/DPP/Icon SMI 547/Newscom; **64:** (t) Arkadiusz Stachowski/Thinkstock; **65:** (t) Mike Hill/Getty Images; **66–67:** (f) Valdrin Xhemaj/epa/Corbis; **68:** (t) © Vivid Pixels/Shutterstock.com; **68:** (t) Leslie Banks/Thinkstock; **68:** (t) FRITZ HOFFMANN/National Geographic Creative; **68:** (t) kali9/Thinkstock; **68:** (l) Patrick Wittmannl/Getty Images; **69:** (t) Andrew Zarivny/Thinkstock; **70:** (t) Gianluca Colla/National Geographic Creative; **70:** (l) Gianluca Colla/National Geographic Creative; **72:** (t) Stephen St. John/National Geographic Creative; **72:** (m) Huntstock/Thinkstock, © StockLite/Shutterstock.com, Robert Ellis/Getty Images, Tom Cockrem/Getty Images, Jacob Wackerhausen/Thinkstock, © DNF Style/Shutterstock.com; **73:** (t) moodboard/Thinkstock; **73:** (b) ML Harris/Getty Images; **75:** (tl, tr, c, bl, br) TED; **76:** (t) Doug Pensinger/Getty Images; **77:** (t) Thomas Mukoya/Reuters/Corbis; **78:** (t) © Maxx-Studio/Shutterstock.com; **79:** (t) James Duncan Davidson/TED; **79:** (2,3,4) TED; **81:** (t) Martin Harvey/Getty Images; **82–83:** (f) David Yoder/National Geographic Creative; **84:** (t) Shafiqul Alam/Demotix/Corbis, Stockbyte/Thinkstock,

radu_m/Thinkstock, Jeffrey Hamilton/Getty Images; **85:** (b) Amy White & Al Petteway/National Geographic Creative; **86:** (t) PAUL CHESLEY/National Geographic Creative; **86:** (l) James Forte/National Geographic Creative; **88:** (t) Kazuyoshi Nomachi/Corbis; **89:** (m) © Jorge Salcedo/Shutterstock.com; **90–91:** (f) Matteo Colombo/Getty Images; **91:** (t) Robb Kendrick/National Geographic Creative; **92:** (t) Tony C French/Getty Images; **93:** (t) Ales Kramer/Getty Images; **94–95:** (f) EIKO JONES; **96:** (t) Ralph Lee Hopkins/National Geographic Creative; **97:** (b) George F. Mobley/National Geograhic Creative; **98:** (t) Brian J. Skerry/National Geographic Creative; **100:** (t) Darlyne A. Murawski/National Geographic Creative; **100:** (t) Stefan Lundgren/National Geographic Creative; **100:** (t) Joel Sartore/National Geographic Creative; **101:** (t) © Lars Christensen/Shutterstock.com; **102:** (b) Ivan Lieman/AFP/Getty Images; **103:** (t) James Duncan Davidson/TED; **104:** (t) Frans Lanting/National Geogrphic Creative; **104:** (c) Gilbert M. Grosvenor/National Geographic Creative; **104:** (b) Martin Harvey/Gallo Images/Getty Images; **105:** (t) Frans Lanting/National Geographic Creative; **106–107:** (f) © Colby Brown Photography; **108:** (t) UIG/Getty Images; **108:** (m) JAMES L. STANFIELD/National Geographic Creative; **108:** (b) Chris Hellier/Alamy; **109:** (m) DAVID HISER/National Geographic Creative; **110:** (t) ERIKA LARSEN/REDUX; **111:** (b) Keenpress/National Geographic Creative; **112:** (t) Paul Nicklen/National Geographic Creative; **113:** (t) Norbert Rosing/Getty Images; **114:** (t) JONATHAN IRISH/National Geographic Creative; **115:** (f) Timothy Allen/Getty Images; **116:** (t) KENT KOBERSTEEN/National Geographic Creative; **117:** (t) CENGAGE/National Geographic Creative; **118:** (t) Beverly Joubert/National Geographic Creative; **119:** (t) James Duncan Davidson/TED; **119:** (1) Beverly Joubert/National Geographic Creative; **119:** (2) Beverly Joubert/National Geographic Creative; **119:** (3) Beverly Joubert/National Geographic Creative; **119:** (4) Beverly Joubert/National Geographic Creative; **121:** (t) Beverly Joubert/National Geographic Creative; **122–123:** (f) Frans Lanting/National